# Outcry
## In The
# Barrio

By
Freddie and Ninfa García

Library of Congress Catalog Number: 87-91109

ISBN: 0-9619319-0-6

PRINTED IN THE UNITED STATES OF AMERICA

This book is true, but certain names have been changed in order to protect the privacy of individuals involved.

*Published by*

Freddie García Ministries
P.O. Box 37387
San Antonio, Texas 78237

# Dedication

This book is dedicated in loving gratitude:

To the memory of Papa and Mama–who raised me with love and understanding, and never gave up on me.

To my wife, Ninfa – the Bible says, "Who can find a virtuous woman? For her price is far above rubies. The heart of her husband doth safely trust in her...She will do him good and not evil all the days of her life...A woman that feareth the Lord, she shall be praised."[1] Who can find a virtuous woman? Papa found a virtuous woman, and so–thank God–did I. To me, Ninfa, you are the virtuous woman described in the Bible.

To my beloved children, Frankie, Ricky, Sandra, Jesse, Josie, Paul, and Jubal–I love each of you very much. The Bible says, "Behold, children are a gift of the Lord; the fruit of the womb is a reward. Like arrows in the hand of a warrior, so are the children of one's youth. How blessed is the man whose quiver is full of them...."[2] My prayer is that each of you will love and serve Jesus Christ and will heed the words of the Lord to Jeremiah: "Thus says the Lord, 'Let not a wise man boast of his wisdom, and let not the mighty man boast of his might, let not a rich man boast of his riches; but let him who boasts boast of this, that he understands and knows Me, that I am the Lord who exercises lovingkindness, justice, and righteousness on earth; for I delight in these things,' declares the Lord."[3]

---

[1] Proverbs 31:10-12, 30b (KJV)

[2] Psalm 127:3-5 (NASB)

[3] Jeremiah 9:23,24 (NASB)

# Acknowledgement

Special thanks to my niece Isabel "Lizzy" García Garay for her patience and faithfulness in typing and retyping the manuscript through its many stages of development.

To Sarah Jorunn Ricketts who would not write the book for us but taught us the craft of writing instead. She discipled us for twelve years through the process of creating this manuscript from the first draft through the final rewrite.

To the entire Victory Fellowship family for their prayers and support.

To Ramón Vásquez y Sánchez for creating the cover.

We also express our appreciation to Paul Annan for providing his knowledge and help in guiding us through the process of preparing the manuscript for publication. He spent many hours at the computer entering the manuscript in preparation for typesetting.

To Bob Jernigan of Creative Typography, Tyler, who worked with us in overseeing the typography and sharing his experience in book publishing to see us through this final stage prior to printing.

# Table of Contents

# Foreword
## By David Wilkerson

Of the writing of biographies—there is no end. After a while, they all seem to run together, especially the life stories of converted addicts and criminals.

Here is a book that stands out vividly among them all. It is high drama and the reader will find it hard to put the book down until the final page.

Freddie and Ninfa have truly sought to glorify Christ in retelling their miraculous life story. I believe that is why it has such power to it. I believe that many who suffer from drug addiction, alcoholism and other life-controlling problems will be saved through reading this marvelous story. It is a book you can give to unconverted friends or family members, knowing it will impact their lives.

I have known Freddie and Ninfa for years and they have proven by their manner of life and Christian witness that theirs is more than just a story—it is an ever-increasing miracle of God's grace!

Freddie is now known lovingly as BISHOP to the many former drug addicts and alcoholics who are pastors of churches. He is truly a father in Zion who, by his life and dedication to Jesus Christ, has set forth an example of integrity and selflessness which is rare today.

The reader of this book is in for an exciting encounter with the power of God. Fasten your seatbelts, and get ready for an emotional roller-coaster ride, because you are going to weep, laugh and rejoice in the almighty grace of Jesus Christ!

His bondservant,

DAVID WILKERSON
Author of *The Cross and the Switchblade*

# Chapter 1

# I Wanna Be Me

For You created my inmost being;
  You knit me together in my mother's womb.
I praise You because I am fearfully
  and wonderfully made;
  Your works are wonderful,
  I know that full well.
My frame was not hidden from You
  when I was made in the secret place.
When I was woven together
  in the depths of the earth,
Your eyes saw my unformed body.
All the days ordained for me
  were written in Your book
  before one of them came to be.

Psalm 139:13-16 (NIV)

San Antonio, Texas, March 1981—The twenty-one gun salute fractured the silence of the cemetery. Then, from the distance came the familiar bugle call of taps, a soldier's farewell to one of his own, and I could no longer hold back my tears.

The six soldiers of the honor guard removed the flag from the coffin and folded it. One of them turned sharply and stepped towards me: "Mr. García, on behalf of the President of the United States, the Commander of the Armed Forces, and the people of this proud nation, we present this flag as a token of services rendered by your loved one."

In a half daze, I took the flag and held it tightly. I could almost hear Papa's voice as he told of defending his country on the battlefields of World War I. He and his two brothers had actually left their plows in the field to enlist in the Army as soon as the news of the war reached their small community of San Marcos, Texas.

As a boy, I had never tired of listening to the stories of combat—the fears, the struggles, the victories. I thrilled to share Papa's pride in having served as a soldier under the American flag. He loved our country and had always instilled in us that America was the best. Where else on the face of the earth could poor people like us fulfill our dreams and reach the highest level of education?

\*       \*       \*

...How well I remember that September day in 1944 when I first went to school, waking to the smell of freshly brewed coffee and refried beans, with the familiar sound of Mama's rolling pin hitting the table as she flattened the dough for our breakfast *tortillas*.[a]

Bright rays of morning sun shone through the cracks between the upright boards in the wall, and my heart beat faster with excitement as my eyes fell on the new overalls, shirt, and shoes waiting for me. Mama had bought them at a secondhand store. She had put aside pennies from the money she made washing and ironing for others, hiding her savings in a bag under sacks of beans and potatoes in a wooden bin in the kitchen. My older brother Chito had shined

---

[a] *tortilla* – a thin, unleavened pancake characteristic of Mexican cookery

the shoes 'til they looked like new. Papa had even taught me how to tie the shoelaces.

I was the youngest of seven children born to Feliciano and Josefa García. We lived on the east side of San Antonio in a *barrio*[b] of mostly Mexican-Americans, with a few Black families. Our two-room house faced a narrow gravel alley off Olive Street. There were eight, identical rental houses sharing a dirt backyard with two outdoor toilets and one water faucet.

I was born in the house, and now I was six—old enough at last to leave home on my own, old enough to begin school. How I wanted to learn to read books, to write, to speak English—even though Papa and Mama had never learned to speak it very well.

Eagerly I jumped up from my blanket on the floor and got dressed. My older brothers and sisters were getting up as well. I folded my blankets and stacked them with theirs in the corner. In the daytime our sleeping quarters became our living room.

Papa was already at the table in the kitchen drinking his cup of coffee with *pan de dulce*.[c] When I walked in, he smiled and announced, "The man of the house is up." He held out his arms, "Come my son, sit here with me."

As I climbed on his lap, Papa turned to Mama and chuckled, "Get the man of the house some coffee."

"No," she objected, "Alfredo's too little."

"Get him his cup of coffee, Mama," Papa insisted. "He's a *macho*.[d]"

---

[b] *barrio* – neighborhood

[c] *pan de dulce* – Mexican pastry

[d] *macho* – an all-around man with the manly traits of honor and dignity

Today was special. Papa had missed work just for me, and now Mama poured some black coffee in a heavy, white mug like Papa's. She added a spoonful of sugar and set it before me, shaking her head a little. But she smiled and urged me, "Hurry up, or you'll be late for your first day of school."

I sipped the strong, sweet brew and gulped my breakfast. Mama handed me my homemade *tacos*[e] for lunch as she shoved us both out the door.

With my hand safely in Papa's, we walked together the nine blocks to Ben Milam Elementary and all the way to my assigned room. Some of the children were crying, but Papa had already explained to me that there was nothing to fear.

As he turned to leave, I tugged at his pants, "Will you come to take me home?"

He grinned and tousled my hair, "Sure, son, I'll be back for you when school is out."

Papa spoke to the teacher in his broken English, and then he was gone. When all of the parents had left, we kids stared at each other not knowing what to expect.

The teacher began talking to us. Her voice was pleasant and she smiled a lot, but to my horror I couldn't understand a word. I waited for her to explain in Spanish but she never did. My heart was pounding, my hands got moist, and I felt my stomach tighten in fear.

Around me the other children seemed to listen intently to the teacher. Did they all understand her? Some of my friends from the *barrio* had a blank expression on their faces, but when the teacher and

---

[e] *tacos* – flour tortillas with various fillings

the Anglo children laughed, my friends laughed too. I felt miserably lost and didn't dare to move 'til the school bell rang and all the children lined up for recess.

Outside in the yard, I was relieved to hear the janitor speak Spanish. But back in the classroom my fear returned. I hid it, and when the teacher and the other children laughed, I did, too.

"Well, son," Papa asked when he picked me up that afternoon, "how was your first day in school?"

"Okay, Papa." I didn't look at him.

When we got home, Mama was outside with a bucket watering her plants, waiting for us. "Did you like school?" she asked.

Knowing how happy they were about my going, I lied, "Yes, Mama."

The next day, through an interpreter, our teacher explained, "If you ever need to use the bathroom, just say, 'Teacher, may I be excused to go to the bathroom?'"

For a Spanish-speaking six-year-old, it was a hard sentence to remember. Later when my friend Ricardo spoke up, he jumbled the words, "Teacher, may I go to the bath excuse?" The English-speaking children bent over with laughter, making all the *barrio* children blush in shame. I felt the sting of humiliation even though I hadn't said a word.

A few days later, I needed to go to the bathroom during class. I wanted desperately to speak but was afraid that the Anglo children would laugh at my broken English. In growing anguish I waited for the bell to ring, but it came too late. My cheeks burned as my classmates put their fingers over their noses and moved their chairs away from me. How embarrassed I was when the teacher took me aside and in a soft voice spoke words I could not understand.

In the end she called the janitor to interpret. With a sympathizing nod, he asked me in Spanish, "Did you go potty in your pants?"

Nearly in tears, I bowed my head.

Patting my shoulder he spoke kindly, "Don't cry, your teacher says that you may go home and change."

At home I told Mama what had happened. I expected her to get upset, but she didn't. As she helped me wash up and change my clothes, I pleaded, "Please, Mama, don't ever make me go back to school again."

"What!" she said sternly. "You listen to me, Alfredo. You will go to school, and you will learn your English. When you grow up, you'll be able to compete in getting a good-paying job. Did you hear me?"

By the firmness of her voice, I knew the issue was closed. Somehow I must learn to survive in school. And gradually, as the months passed, the strange sounds of another language began to make sense. I could separate words, even speak them.

\*　　　　\*　　　　\*

In the second grade we started learning songs such as "God Bless America," and I had memorized the "Pledge of Allegiance" by heart, even if I didn't understand it all. But during recess, we Mexican-American kids played together and naturally spoke our own language.

One day the teacher suddenly brought our game to a halt. She summoned two Anglo boys who were playing nearby and put her arms around them. Then she turned to us, "Don't you know, that it's rude to speak in another language in front of someone who doesn't understand? You can hurt that person's feelings; besides, you're living in America, and in America our language is English. In fact, you're all Americans and should speak nothing but English."

Pointing to the nearest Mexican-American girl, she added, "María, from now on your name will be Mary; Rogelio, you'll be Roger." The teacher went on and on until she came to me. "Alfredo, what would you like to be called? Fred or Freddie?"

I shrugged my shoulders, "It doesn't matter."

"Then Fred it is," she nodded. "From now on anyone caught speaking Spanish on the school grounds will be punished. You will either be spanked or detained after school."

That day I determined to practice my English more diligently at home as well as at school, but Mama quickly stopped me.

"No, Alfredo," she wagged her finger in front of my face, "you practice your English in school. At recess when you are playing with your Spanish-speaking friends, it's all right to speak Spanish, but whenever English-speaking persons who don't understand Spanish are present, you speak English out of respect. Here at home, you practice your Spanish. That way, my son, you'll be able to speak both languages."

"But Mama," I argued, "our teacher told us that we're Americans and that Americans speak English, not Spanish."

She sat me beside her. "Your teacher is right," she explained. "You are an American because you were born here in the United States. But you're an American of Mexican descent. If you lose your Spanish language completely, son, you'll be losing a part of what God created you to be.

"Besides," she added, "your Papa and I don't speak English very well, so for our benefit, here in the house, you'll speak Spanish."

Instinctively I knew that Mama was right. But at the same time I yearned to win the approval of my teacher and be accepted as an equal by my English-speaking classmates.

\*　　　　\*　　　　\*

In third grade our teacher hung a chart next to the blackboard and announced: "On this chart I'll record the names of the students with the highest grades. They will receive a gold star. Those who earn the second-highest grades will get a silver star."

I eagerly accepted the challenge. *I'm gonna get that gold star and get my name up there*, I said to myself. *I know I can do it!*

The first time the names went up, I searched down the list with anticipation. My heart sank when I saw that only names of Anglo children had stars.

"That's all right," I consoled myself. "I'll try harder and make it next time." But when the next list went up, my name was not on it. Still I tried again and again, and with each failure my hopes sank and my doubts grew. *Perhaps it's really true that Mexican-Americans are dumb*, I thought.

That evening Mama walked into the bedroom and caught me in front of the mirror. "Alfredo!" she screamed. "What are you doing?" Grabbing a damp cloth, she rushed to my side and began removing the white powder I had put all over my face.

"I want to be white, Mama," I fought back the tears, "'cause I want to be smart like the White kids."

"Son," her warm, dark eyes were moist, "your beautiful brown skin has nothing to do with your being dumb or smart. It's how much time you spend studying."

"But Mama!" I insisted, "I do study. I study real hard, but still the Anglo kids are the only ones who get the little gold stars. The *gabachitos*[f] always know the answers."

She shook her head with a tender smile, "You're not dumb, Alfredo; it only seems like it because the little Anglo children had an advantage over you from the first day in school. They are taught in their own language."

I was not convinced. "Then how come that in all the books I've seen in school, there's no Mexican-Americans?"

She looked as if she wanted to explain but instead put her arm around me. "I'll tell you what, son. I'm gonna ask your sisters Estella and Aurora–whenever they're home from work early–to help you study to better your grades. Now, let's go into the kitchen and I'll make you a *tortilla*."

Seated at the table watching Mama work, I felt happy and secure once again. The kerosene lamp threw a warm circle of light over the plank floor and bare, wooden walls, scrubbed spotlessly clean. Mama had made cheerful curtains of flour sack material for the windows. Behind the cast-iron cook stove was the neat pile of logs Papa and I had cut and stacked that morning.

I watched Mama's skillful hands as she rolled out the *tortillas* and slapped them on the hot stove top.

---

[f] *gabachitos* – White kids

The aroma of *tortillas* cooking, the crackling of the wood burning, and the soft light of the lamp made me feel warm inside.

Tomorrow in school I would try again to study harder.

\*   \*   \*

Our fourth-grade teacher was Mrs. Emery, and I liked her from the start. She closed the classroom door carefully before greeting us the first day in school.

"You Mexican-American children are very lucky in that you're learning two languages," she smiled at us. "We Anglos speak only English, both at school and at home. Your cultural upbringing offers you the opportunity of being bilingual."

In our class of thirty students, we Mexican-Americans were the majority. Now I grinned at my friends and relaxed in my seat. This promised to be a good year.

Mrs. Emery's history classes were especially fun. We studied the cultures of early American Indians. We learned to make drums out of rubber tire tubes and old coffee cans and how to make teepees, bows, and arrows. On one memorable day, our teacher brought a real Indian in native dress who danced for us. Soon, we were all playing "Cowboys and Indians" and everyone wanted to be Indians.

"You Mexican-Americans have Indian blood flowing through your veins," Mrs. Emery told us. "And the Indians knew how to live off the land. They did not destroy plants or animals just for fun. They hunted only to provide food, clothing, and shelter for their families."

My heart pounded with excitement all the way home. That evening when Papa came from work, I asked him, "Do we really have Indian blood in us?"

"*Sí*,ᵏ" he smiled. "We have both Indian and Spanish blood. Right, Mama?"

"*Es verdad*–That's true," she nodded. "Many years ago when the Spaniards conquered the Indians of Mexico, our race was born."

Mrs. Emery's lessons and my parents' explanation made me feel important. It felt good to know I was special. But I was in for a cruel disappointment.

Television was a luxury we couldn't afford, but our neighbor, Mrs. Zúñiga, bought the first TV in the *barrio* and invited all of the neighborhood kids to watch.

There we saw our first Western movies, but to my dismay, Indians were always uncivilized savages who always lost to the White man in the end. My friends and I were embarrassed when we heard the Lone Ranger insult his Indian companion by calling him "Tonto"–the word for "dummy" in Spanish. From then on when we played, none of us wanted to be *tontos*; we all wanted to be the Lone Ranger.

\*　　　　\*　　　　\*

In the fifth grade came another blow to my self-image.

"I need to fill in some reports," Mrs. Johnson announced. "As I call your name, tell me what your father does for a living.

---

ᵏ *Sí* – yes

"Harold?"

"My father is an insurance man."

"Patty?"

"He's a salesman."

"Arturo?"

"He works in anything, ma'am," he muttered shyly.

"Yes, Arturo," she spoke distinctly, "but what is his trade?"

All eyes were focused on Arturo who had turned red and squirmed. "I don't know, ma'am," he barely whispered. "He digs ditches, and..." By now the entire class was giggling.

The teacher realized her mistake. Unintentionally, she had made Arturo a laughingstock. She tried to make amends and told the class to be quiet.

"Your father is a laborer, Arturo; that's nothing to be ashamed of. He works with his hands."

But the damage was done.

As she continued calling out names, I was in mental anguish: *What will I say or how can I say it? They're gonna laugh at me, too.* Just then, she called my name, "Freddie?"

I wanted to hide. "He's a janitor, ma'am." My voice was barely audible, and I hunched my shoulders as the wave of surrounding laughter engulfed me.

"I'll show them," I promised myself. "I'll never let a teacher embarrass me again."

At home, I told my brother Chito. But he quickly warned me, "You better not mess up in Mrs. Johnson's class; she'll get the paddle to you."

Mama overheard Chito's remark. "That's good," she nodded her approval. "If you don't do as you're told, Alfredo, you deserve to be spanked. I believe that if teachers sacrifice their time to educate and help raise my children, they also have the right to spank you when you misbehave or don't mind."

Mrs. Johnson was true to her reputation. She demanded that our homework be completed on time. "Learn to read and write!" she insisted. "You don't want to spend all your life digging ditches. It's a job, but you can do better with an education."

Mama was pleased with my teacher, but I thought Mrs. Johnson was mean. She even looked like Miss Grundy, the strict teacher in *Archie* comic books. One day before class I drew Miss Grundy's picture on the blackboard and wrote our teacher's name underneath. I signed it: "By Doug." He was an Anglo boy who lived near us. We often walked home from school together and sometimes stopped to play along the way.

The drawing was a great hit in class. Everyone was laughing when Mrs. Johnson walked in. "Doug! Did you do that?" Her face was stern but a quiver in her voice betrayed her hurt.

"No, ma'am."

"But you do know who drew it, don't you?"

Doug avoided her eyes and shook his head.

Looking at each of us in turn, she spoke firmly, "I want to know by tomorrow who's responsible for this."

On our way home from school, Doug caught up with me. "Why did you put my name? I'm gonna have to tell her it was you who did it."

I remained silent, but in my mind I was scheming how to stop him. When we came to my house, I asked him to stay a while.

"Are you home from school, Alfredo?" Mama called from the kitchen where she and Papa were having coffee.

"Yes, Mama. I'm home already."

On the back porch was the rope swing Papa had

made for me, tied to an overhead beam.

"Your turn first," I offered Doug.

Grinning happily, he stepped up to seat himself in the loop.

"Wait a minute, I need to fix the ropes," I called out and jumped up on a chair to reach the knot. Doug was unsuspecting. Quickly I untied one side of the swing and held on to the loose rope-end hanging over the beam. With my other hand, I rapidly swung the rope around Doug's neck and started to pull.

"I'm gonna hang you so you don't tell the teacher who did it!"

"No! No!" Doug gasped, his eyes filled with terror.

"Alfredo, leave him alone!" Mama screamed and rushed to grab me.

I let go of the rope. Papa quickly removed the loop from Doug's neck and told him, "Go home, run! ¡Pronto![h]"

Doug fled down the driveway.

Without another word Papa removed his belt, and I knew I had it coming. After the spanking, Papa and Mama demanded to know why I wanted to kill Doug.

I told them the truth.

"But why did you put Doug's name on your drawing?" Mama asked.

"I figured that since he is an Anglo, they wouldn't punish him."

"Oh, Alfredo." She shook her head in distress. "You would be punished not because you're a Mexican-American but because you had done wrong."

I never knew if Doug told, but Mrs. Johnson did not mention the incident again.

\*            \*            \*

---

[h] ¡Pronto! – hurry

That year when summer came, Papa and Mama, Chito, María, and I went as migrant workers to the cotton fields. My aunt and uncle and all my cousins came too. We worked long, hard hours from early morning to sunset, but on Saturdays and Sundays we found time for fishing, rabbit hunting, and swimming in a water hole. It was so much fun that the hard work didn't matter.

Papa got our paycheck on Saturday, and we'd all go to town. Papa and my uncle had a few beers while Mama and *Tía Cata*[i] did the shopping. We kids got to go to the movie house. One Saturday when we were in town, Papa suggested we eat supper at a restaurant. At the front door, we were stopped by an Anglo man. "You can't come in here; this café is for White folks. You wanna eat, go around the back. We have a place for Mexicans and Blacks there."

Papa patiently tried to explain, "I'm American. I've got money."

"You're not White, sir," the man was annoyed. "Go out back."

"What did he say?" Mama asked.

"He says we're not White and to go eat out back with the Blacks," I translated.

"How come no one asked what color Papa was when he went to war?" Mama's voice faltered. "Mexican-Americans are the first to be drafted and placed in the front lines. Alfredo," she gestured, "tell him in English what I said."

Before I could say a word, Papa stopped me. "Be quiet, Alfredo; he doesn't understand."

I bit my lip to keep from crying, but anger was churning inside me. It was an incident I swore never

---

[i] *Tía Cata* – Aunt Katherine

to forget.

*             *             *

Back in school that fall, my attitude had hardened.

"Speak English, Freddie!" My sixth-grade teacher called me to attention.

"*¿Qué dijiste?*[j]" I replied insolently.

Around me the Mexican-American children giggled, and the teacher warned: "Quiet! Or I'll keep all of you after school." I smiled triumphantly as the bell rang. One round for me.

A couple of days later in history class, the teacher asked, "Who discovered America?"

"I believe the Indians discovered Columbus," I answered. The entire class began laughing.

The teacher's face reddened. She ignored me, turned to Jeffrey, and repeated, "Who discovered America?"

"Columbus, ma'am."

"Very good," she complimented him.

Turning again towards the Mexican-American students she asked, "What are the names of Columbus' three ships?"

None of us answered and she implored, "Come on, let's all participate. If you don't get the right answer, that's all right; we're here to learn."

We all avoided her eyes. Julio began to write in his notebook; Sergio put his head on his arms and pretended to sleep; Chemo dropped his pencil on the floor and stooped to find it; I stared intently out the window.

The poor teacher didn't realize that no matter how nicely she asked, we would not respond. As for me, I

---

[j] *¿Qué dijiste?* – What did you say?

refused to be humiliated or laughed at ever again.

After my last day in sixth grade, I came home to a familiar scene. In the backyard stood a washtub full of water and crushed ice, holding two, big watermelons bobbing against each other. The third watermelon had already been cut up, and my whole family was there munching on it while they listened to Spanish *polcas*[k] on the radio.

"Here," Mama said, handing me a piece of cold melon.

Just then Papa motioned, "Come sit beside me, Alfredo. I wanna talk to you."

He was serious, and I squirmed nervously. *What did Papa know?*

"Your brother Chito tells me that the boys from the Austin Street Gang are smoking marijuana," he looked at me searchingly. "I don't want you hanging around with gangs, especially not them. Get yourself some good friends when you start Emerson Junior High this fall."

I bit into the watermelon to escape his eyes. Papa didn't realize that his counsel was too late. I had already chosen my friends among the *batos locos*[l]– Benny, Mario, Pancho, Rudy, and Flaco. They were *chicanos*[m] like me, proud of our Mexican heritage, not ashamed of our language and culture. Already, we had formed our own teenage Austin Street Gang.

---

[k] *polcas* – polkas

[l] *batos locos* – crazy guys or cool guys

[m] *chicano* – a U.S. citizen of Mexican descent born in the United States

# Chapter 2

# Los Batos Locos[a]

Hear, my son, your father's instruction,
   And do not forsake your mother's teaching.

Proverbs 1:8 (NASB)

A wise son makes a father glad,
   But a foolish son is a grief to his mother.

Proverbs 10:1 (NASB)

"Hey, Carmen!" Flaco yelled. "Put some money in the juke box."

When the rock and roll music filled the Van Ness Drug Store, *chicanos*[b] from the *barrio*[c] began dancing up and down the aisles.

"Stop it!" Andy, the owner, yelled. "You know you're not supposed to dance in here!" No one listened, and Andy shook his head. "What's the use? I give up."

Pancho and I had been ignoring the scene. Now we stepped outside just in time to see Yolanda, a girl from our *barrio*, walking down the street holding hands with an Anglo guy.

"Hey, Yolanda!" we both hollered, "you run out of beans?"

She turned with a smirk, "Shut up you Mexicans!"

"Hey, Freddie, check this girl out," Pancho spoke

---

[a] Los Batos Locos – the crazy guys or the cool guys

[b] *chicano* – a U.S. citizen of Mexican descent born in the United States

[c] *barrio* – neighborhood

loud enough for her to hear. "Yolanda is blacker than some of our soul sisters in the *barrio*, yet she thinks she's White."

"Yeah," I teased, "she looks like she works at cleaning chimneys."

"Ha! Ha! Ha!" everyone around us jeered. But I felt rage rise within me. I wanted to grab that cocky *gringo*[d] and beat him up good—teach him and that turncoat Yolanda a lesson.

"I'd like to smear her precious White status symbol on the sidewalk and spit on him," I muttered.

Benny, Mario, Rudy, and Flaco had joined Pancho and me. They had heard my remark. Rudy spat after Yolanda and her boyfriend as they turned the corner, "Come on, Freddie, cut them loose, they ain't no big thing. Let's go get loaded. I can talk Sleepy into giving me three *grifos*[e] for a buck."

I had already tried drinking beer and sniffing paint thinner and gasoline with the gang. But this was different. I hesitated, remembering Papa's warning, *"Don't ever smoke marijuana, Alfredo."*

"Come on, Freddie," Pancho nudged me, "there's nothing to be afraid of. Pot[f] isn't like heroin that you get hooked on. You can take it or leave it."

We all walked towards the pusher's[g] home, but when we got to Lockwood Park, Rudy stopped. "You wait here. If Sleepy sees everyone, he might panic and not let me have any."

He walked into a house across the street and soon

---

[d] *gringo* – a White male person

[e] *grifos* – marijuana cigarettes

[f] pot – marijuana

[g] pusher – person who sells drugs

returned grinning from ear to ear. In his hand were six, slim, hand-rolled marijuana cigarettes. Opening both ends of one, he lit it and took several drags, holding the smoke in his lungs as long as possible. Then he passed the cigarette to me.

Following his example, I inhaled deeply and held my breath. Within seconds, it hit me; I started feeling like I was the smartest *chicano* in the *barrio*. From now on, nobody could tell me that marijuana was bad. Man, I fell in love with pot.

Within weeks I learned to keep my cool under the influence. No one could tell I was loaded, and I started going high to school. The drug gave me new confidence. I was really one of the cool cats now, accepted by my peers–but I was not satisfied. I wanted to be admired by everyone, to be looked up to, to feel the high of popularity. I saw just one small problem but was embarrassed to mention it to Mama.

One afternoon, however, after making sure she was alone at home, I walked into the kitchen, grabbed a piping hot *tortilla*[h] off the griddle, and sat down at the table. I tried to act casual. "Mama, can I go to the store and buy some bread and bologna for my school lunch tomorrow?"

"Bread?" she was surprised. "Don't you like the *tacos*[i] I make for you?"

"Yes, Mama," I assured her, "especially the ones with Mexican sausage and refried beans. But when we take homemade *tacos*, the fellows at school laugh at us."

---

[h] *tortilla* – a thin, unleavened pancake characteristic of Mexican cookery

[i] *tacos* – flour tortillas with various fillings

"Who laughs at you?" She looked hurt. "Is it the Anglos?"

"No, Mama! The White kids like my *tacos*. They always want me to trade them for their ham sandwiches." My hands were sweating, and I added nervously, "The truth is, Mama—it's Mexican-American guys who make fun of us. They don't really laugh to my face, but I've seen them make fun behind Pedro's back because his parents can't afford to buy him sandwiches."

"Well, they're crazy," she scoffed. "How come they laugh? Aren't *tortillas* what they eat at home? Isn't that what their parents eat? Beans, *chile*,[j] and *tortillas*?"

"Please, Mama," I pleaded. "May I go get some bread and bologna at the store?"

"You know, Alfredo," she wagged her finger at me, "you have to wait 'til Papa gets home to ask his permission."

How well I knew that with a big family to feed, every penny was needed. But surprisingly enough, when I asked him, Papa said yes.

Many times after that, I sat beside Pedro at school, eating sandwiches while he munched happily on his *taco*. My mouth watered for the taste of *tortillas* and beans, but I didn't dare ask for a bite. What if somebody saw me—and laughed.

One Saturday night, near the end of the school year, I was goofing around with some friends at the drug store. Benny and Rudy drove up in a shiny, new car.

"Get in!" Rudy yelled. "Let's go joy riding."

---

[j] *chile* – hot pepper

The gang and I crowded into the back seat. Rudy handed each of us a joint,[k] and Benny stepped on the gas. We smelled burned rubber as the tires spun against the asphalt. It was great! When Mario discovered a full whiskey bottle in the back seat, we all cheered.

Benny was the only experienced driver, and he offered to teach us. Each had a turn at the wheel, and with each lesson the car received more dents and scratches.

I'd never been behind a steering wheel, and when my turn came, Rudy objected. "Freddie's too wild; he'll blow it, man."

"I'm next!" I yelled. "You've already had your chance."

Rudy gave in, and I pushed the gas pedal to the floor. The car swerved dangerously as I tried to maneuver around a curb. We bounced onto the sidewalk and laughed uproariously as I managed to sideswipe a parked car on our way back to the street.

"There's a cop following us!" Mario hollered in my ear.

"I told you that Freddie would blow it," Rudy grumbled.

Instantly Benny took command. "Slide over, Freddie," he ordered calmly. "Let me drive."

Within minutes there were four squad cars on our tail with sirens blaring. But with Benny at the wheel, we knew we could beat them.

For the next half hour the thrill of the chase had us jumping, laughing, and cheering as Benny took us on a wild ride through back alleys, side streets, and

---

[k] joint – a marijuana cigarette

across the cemetery. Behind us were the swirling, red lights and screaming sirens, just like in the movies. I felt the surge of exhilaration and thought nothing of the danger 'til Benny slammed on the brakes in an alley and yelled, "Every man for himself. It's a dead end!" Swinging the doors open, we all took off in different directions before the police got there.

From then on, stealing cars became part of our lifestyle. We drove them 'til they ran out of gas, then stripped them of all we could sell before dumping them. The money gave us independence, all the booze[1] and pot we wanted, and change for the juke box and the movies. Our favorites were the gangster movies, and my heroes were Al Capone, Lucky Luciano, Arnold Rothstein, and John Dillinger.

Soon people put pressure on the police to stop the bunch of *chicanos* who were vandalizing the community. Cops began patrolling the drug store more frequently, taking us down to Juvenile Hall for questioning whenever they saw the gang together. But they never caught us red-handed and couldn't prove their suspicions.

One day Mario and I were walking down Austin Street when a cop named Cleto Sánchez stopped us. "We've been getting all kinds of complaints," he warned us. "This is my beat now. I better not catch any of you yellow punks hanging around these street corners. Is that understood?"

Immediately the word went out among the gang that the drug store was taboo 'til things cooled off. Instead, we hung out at the Hot Corner, a nearby beer joint, playing pool and listening to the juke box. After

---

[1] booze – alcoholic beverages

a few days, Mario and I got bored and decided to see what was happening at the drug store.

The place turned out to be dead. We stood on the corner debating what to do next when a squad car pulled up. It was Cleto Sánchez.

He got out. "Didn't I tell you bums I didn't want to see you around here?" Opening the back door, he grabbed us both. "Get in, you dirty punks," he sneered. "I'm going to give you a lesson in obedience."

He drove to the deserted football field at Emerson Junior High School, pulled us out of the car, and slowly removed his heavy, leather belt.

"*Cálmala, ese*–Hey, calm down," I tried to reason with him, "*¡Cálmala!*"

"Speak English!" Officer Sánchez shouted as he swung the belt at both of us. "When you talk to me, you speak English!" His face burned with anger, and he lashed at us blindly.

We shielded our faces against his fury as the sting of the leather strap came down on us. Mario and I tried to make a run for it, but Officer Sánchez was quicker. He didn't stop whipping us 'til our arms and backs were covered with bruises.

"Now beat it!" His eyes were dark with hatred. "Don't ever let me catch you again."

Angry tears pressed against my eyelids. To hide my emotions, I turned quickly to walk away. Officer Sánchez was not going to have the satisfaction of seeing me cry.

"Speak English! Speak English!" I mimicked his words. His Spanish accent had been as strong as mine.

"*Se sale*–He's out of line," Mario cursed.

"Look at this," I pulled off my shirt. Ugly welts had

sprung up on my arms and shoulders, and Mario was no better off.

We didn't dare go back to the drug store but, instead, continued to hang out on the patio behind the Hot Corner. There we entertained ourselves tripping out on pot and beer while the juke box blared inside. Bubba ran the Hot Corner's pool hall, and Sally, a sad-looking, old alcoholic, was always there trying to hustle drinks.

One evening we had been looking at pornographic magazines when Bubba shoved Sally out the back door. "Go home, you old whore!" he yelled. "Stop bothering my customers."

Sally staggered past us. Pancho threw the porno magazine to the side, "Let's rape the old hag."

The alley was dark, and all ten of us ganged up on her. Benny pushed her down and placed his foot over her mouth to stop her screaming. Mario and I held her arms while all of us kicked and spat on her.

Wiggling herself out from under Benny's foothold, she pleaded, "Please boys, let me go! Please!"

One of the guys kicked her in the side. "Shut up, honky!ᵐ" he hollered. "Shut up!"

We were making so much noise that before long, dogs started barking and porch lights went on. We ran, leaving Sally sobbing on the ground with her clothes all torn.

The next day we went to school unconcerned, knowing that she had been too drunk to identify any of us.

\*　　　　　\*　　　　　\*

---

ᵐ honky – offensive term for a White person

That fall, I started the ninth grade. Miss Martínez was our Spanish teacher. She was young and beautiful, and all of us guys fell in love with her. It was the only class we all slicked up to look good in, and we were on our best behavior.

"Those of you with English names," Miss Martínez announced, "will be given a Spanish name as part of the Spanish-speaking project. You will answer roll call and address each other by this name during our class: Janie–Juanita, Rodney–Rodrigo, William–Guillermo..."

Each time Miss Martínez named one of the students, several of the Mexican-Americans giggled.

"What's so funny?" she turned to them. "These Spanish names are beautiful. Why do you laugh?"

Some looked embarrassed; others hid behind their blank expressions. No one answered. *Why are they laughing?* I asked myself.

Gradually, as weeks passed, I began to see that many of my Mexican-American classmates were ashamed of their Spanish language and thought a Spanish name was a put-down. Their laughter held scorn for their own cultural heritage. Now I could understand why some of them tried to put on an Anglo accent in pronouncing their own Spanish surname. Like George Rodríguez who called himself "Rah-DREE-gez." To see my people trying to become carbon copies of the Anglo–just to be accepted–made me angry.

"No way, José," I determined. "That ain't for me. No more bologna sandwiches. I don't care who laughs."

Three weeks before graduating from Emerson Junior High, Mario and I were walking home from school when a kid from our *barrio* came running with bad news. "La Loma Gang is waiting for you by the alley," he panted.

A rumble had been brewing between the Austin Street and La Loma Gangs, and we were prepared. Quickly the word was passed to our gang, and the La Loma guys who had planned to catch Mario and me alone were taken by surprise instead.

The narrow alley resounded with shouts as we joined in battle. Just a few of us had weapons: switchblades, clubs, and chains. Some fought with bare fists. The alley was strewn with rocks and gravel, and soon we were hurling stone missiles at each other. All you could hear were the groanings of guys as they were hit. Spectators were terrified as they watched the rumble.

We chased the La Loma Gang off, but when I got home limping, with my shirt torn and blood running from my nose, Mama decided it was time to take action.

A month later she gave me the news, "Alfredo, Papa's made a down payment on a house."

"A house? Where?" I had no desire to leave my east side *barrio*.

"On the west side," she calmly replied.

My heart sank. But like it or not, when school was out for the summer, we moved to our new home across town.

I enrolled in Tech High; however, before the fall semester was over, I dropped out and found a job working night shift at a restaurant.

Soon, I got a car, and on my days off, I headed across town to visit the guys in my old *barrio*. But the distance made a difference; I was no longer involved in the daily activities of the gang. I felt isolated.

One afternoon I was downtown waiting for Mario. My throat was dry and sore from smoking pot, so I walked into the nearest snack bar. A cute waitress was behind the counter, and I asked her name.

"Alice," she smiled. "May I help you?"

I'd always been shy around girls. In fact, I had never tried to date because I felt sure that no girl would ever give me a second look. But Alice was different. She seemed to like me. We talked easily, and when I offered to drive her home after work, she accepted.

In the days that followed we saw each other as often as we could. Alice was my first sweetheart, and I was no longer alone. Three months later, when she was seventeen and I was eighteen, we got married.

I eagerly accepted my responsibility as a husband and worked hard at being a good provider. My parents owned an empty lot on San Eduardo Street and allowed me to build a small, one-bedroom house for us there. I thought I had it made—I had a wife, was buying my own home, and had a good-paying job. It was time to settle down.

My old friends would drop by just to kid me about being the only married guy from the gang. I laughed with them, but I was proud of myself.

When my son, Frankie, was born, I bought a box of cigars and went straight to my *barrio* to celebrate with the gang. Two years later, I did it again when Ricky, my second son, was born. But there was a difference. Benny, Mario, and the rest of the gang had started using heroin.

*Why would they do a crazy thing like that?* I thought to myself. *Man, heroin is the one drug we said we'd never use!*

I didn't go back as often after that; besides, I had

problems of my own. Alice and I had been struggling to keep our relationship from falling apart. We had separated and made up several times. Now in our fifth year of married life, things were getting worse.

To avoid the conflict at home, I hung out in *cantinas*[n] and dance halls 'til the wee hours of the morning. And after the birth of our baby girl, Sandra, Alice gave up. "I'm filing for divorce, Freddie. This time, I'm leaving for good."

---

[n] *cantinas* – beer joints

# Chapter 3

# Monkey on My Back[a]

Jesus answered them, I assure you,
most solemnly I tell you,
Whoever commits and practices sin
is the slave of sin.

John 8:34 (AMP)

The loss of my children and my failure as husband
crushed me. I was twenty-three and lonelier now
than ever before, my dreams and expectations shat-
tered. Trying to forget, I combined drinking hard li-
quor with smoking pot[b] and dropping pills daily.

At the restaurant where I worked was Ninfa, a fun-
loving waitress. She didn't hesitate when I introduced her to marijuana. Under the influence of pot,
she was easily persuaded to spend the night with me,
even when I explained my terms: "I want you to
understand what you're getting into. I'm still hurting over my first marriage, and I never intend to get
married again. So if you're getting any idea about
that, forget it. We can keep house, play house, but
marriage is out."

"I'm game, Freddie," she agreed. "I'll be satisfied
just being with you." Her brown eyes looked sincere,
and she stood on tiptoe to place her hands against my
cheeks. "I'll never leave you, unless you ask me to." I

---

[a] Monkey on My Back – any drug addiction that must be fed,
especially addiction to heroin

[b] pot – marijuana

didn't believe her, but a few days later we moved in together.

Ninfa's attention helped ease my loneliness, but nothing could really take away the pain of separation from my children. Hoping to gain custody of them, I consulted a lawyer. He explained how the law favored the mother in such cases, and I left his office heartbroken.

Back in the car, the realization hit me—I'd never get my kids back. Their childhood years would be lost to me forever. Sobs wracked my body as I drove aimlessly through the streets of San Antonio.

It was late afternoon before I could bear to head for the motel where Ninfa was waiting. Together we drove over to Austin Street and stopped at Benny's house.

"Let's go have a beer at Fernández Bar," I invited him.

"*Vamos*,"[c] Benny was ready.

It wasn't until the third beer that I noticed Benny was sick. He had a look of desperation, his body moving constantly, his nose running. It dawned on me; he needed a fix[d] bad.

Experiencing pain of my own, I took out my wallet and handed him some bills. "Here, Benny, go get some stuff.[e] But after you fix, give me a taste."

"You d-d-drive," he stuttered, snatching the money from my hand.

After scoring,[f] Benny directed us to an empty

---

[c] *Vamos* – Let's go.

[d] fix – an injection of narcotics

[e] stuff – heroin

[f] score – to obtain anything, usually drugs; to purchase drugs

shack in a back lot. He fixed first, then tied my arm with his belt. Ninfa had remained silent, but when she saw I was really serious, she pleaded, "Please, Freddie, don't."

"Shut up and leave me alone; I know what I'm doing," I pushed her away. The needle hurt, and soon I felt the sensation of drowsiness. The next thing I knew I was vomiting.

"Don't worry about it, Freddie," Benny slurred, "I vomited my first time too."

In the beginning I fixed only once a month; then it became weekly, and within six months, I was fixing two times a day.

One afternoon Ninfa and I were in the Hot Corner's backyard having a few beers. Mario and Benny had just scored and were in the bathroom fixing.

"Sure hope they leave some for me," I told Ninfa. "Maybe it'll help my flu." My entire body had been aching all day, and I felt very weak. My eyes were watering, and I was getting cold chills.

Just then, Benny stuck his head out the bathroom door, "Hey, Freddie, you wanna taste?"

"Sure, man!" I grabbed my belt, tightening it around my arm as I walked toward them. As soon as the heroin started flowing through my veins, all my "flu" symptoms disappeared. I didn't want to admit it—but I was really hooked.[g]

The worried look on Ninfa's face cut me to the bone. I patted her belly and tried to smile. "Hey, you're six months pregnant so don'tcha go around worrying. You just take care of yourself. I'm gonna stop, believe

---

[g] hooked – addicted to drugs

me. By the time you have the baby, I'll be back on my feet."

After leaving the Hot Corner, we decided to spend the evening at my parents' home. The instant I walked into the living room, Mama pointed her finger in my face. "Tell me the truth, Alfredo, are you using the needle?"

"Mama!" I pretended surprise, "you know I wouldn't touch that stuff."

"Don't lie to me, Alfredo. Your sister Santos tells me she saw you all doped up." Mama was on the verge of tears, but she choked them back and demanded, "When do you plan to stop?"

Before I could answer, she turned to Ninfa, "I can tell something is wrong. Alfredo was always neat and clean and ate good. Now he goes around filthy and unshaven; he wears the same clothes for days and he eats nothing but sweets."

Ninfa didn't say a word, but we could not fool Mama. She knew me too well. Her hurt made me uncomfortable. "This will be the last time you see me like this, Mama," I promised.

But as the weeks passed, things went from bad to worse. To support the habit, I joined Benny and Mario in burglarizing homes and *carruchas*.[h] Ninfa learned to be the lookout and to drive the get-away car.

One afternoon, as we were cruising around checking the parked cars, Mario shouted, "Look! That station wagon's full of typewriters."

"Let's hit it!" I urged. "*¡Vente!*—Come on!"

We had just finished loading the merchandise when

---

[h] *carruchas* – cars

I heard a man yell, "Stop! Somebody stop them!"

As we sped away, I saw in the rearview mirror that the man jotted down our license number. We sold the equipment *pronto*,[i] got our fix, and left Mario and Benny in the *barrio*.[j] Ninfa and I dumped the car in a deserted spot and took in a movie. After the show, we went directly to the police department and reported the car stolen.

"Don't change your story," I coached Ninfa. "No matter what they ask, we were in the movies and that's all."

Next day Sgt. Ramírez left word at Mama's house that I was wanted at the police station. When I got there, he put it to me bluntly. "Freddie, you know that I know; you stole that equipment and reported the car stolen."

"You're crazy!" I argued. "I'm against stealing!"

"I've got a witness who saw you," he came back. "Are you willing to stand in a line-up?"

"Sure I'll stand," I bluffed. "I ain't got nothing to hide; I was in the movies with my girl."

Some line-up. I was the only one there. Luckily, with my change of clothes and a clean shave, the witness couldn't identify me. "Can I leave now, sergeant?" I smiled broadly.

"You punk!" he was disgusted. "How can you stand there and lie with such a straight face? I'm going to give you enough rope so you can hang yourself. You'll be back."

\*　　　　\*　　　　\*

---

[i] *pronto* – quickly
[j] *barrio* – neighborhood

I made an earnest attempt to kick[k] my habit, but I had lost control of my will power. I had long since lost my job. When we could afford it, Ninfa and I slept in a cheap motel, but more often we spent the night in junked cars, abandoned houses, or outdoors in parks and empty lots. We put flattened cardboard boxes on the ground and covered ourselves with newspaper. Summer was near and we no longer suffered cold and freezing rain, but I worried about Ninfa's health and our baby. Her time to deliver was soon, but she never complained.

When she started in labor, I was glad to drop her off at the twenty-four hour clinic. Afterwards, my aunt took her home. Two weeks passed before I showed up to see my new son.

"I named him Jesse like you wanted," Ninfa proudly announced. I was high on drugs as usual, and she confronted me, "I've been doing some serious thinking, Freddie. What chance does the baby have with us—a junkie father and a weedhead[l] pill-popper for a mother?"

"I've been thinking too," I avoided her eyes. "I don't like the idea of leaving him, but maybe your *madre de crianza*[m] will take care of him just 'til we straighten out."

No more was said about it, but a month after Jesse's birth, we left him with Ninfa's adoptive mother, promising ourselves we'd be back as soon as I kicked my habit once and for all.

\*     \*     \*

---

[k] kick – to withdraw from drugs

[l] weedhead – marijuana user

[m] *madre de crianza* – foster mother or adoptive mother

I lost count of how many times I repeated the cycle of kicking physically and getting hooked again. My body could go through the painful withdrawal from drugs, but my mind remained obsessed with the need for it.

"I have no peace," I tried to explain to Ninfa. "All I can visualize twenty-four hours a day is the eyedropper and the needle. I have the will to change, but I don't have the power."

Our lives became an endless merry-go-round of enslavement to drugs, and when Ninfa got pregnant again, we did not want the responsibility of another child. We could think of only one alternative—abortion.

The midwife had a long waiting list, so Ninfa wasn't treated 'til close to her fifth month of pregnancy. She stayed overnight at the midwife's home, and the next evening I came by to pick her up. I honked in front of the house and Ninfa came out, carrying a small bundle wrapped in newspapers and old rags.

"It was a boy." Her voice was toneless. "Do you want to see him?" She began unwrapping the bundle on the seat between us.

A cold tremor ran down my spine and I yelled: "No! No! Just put it down on the floor. Hide it!"

Ninfa was crying silently beside me, and I tried to avoid thinking of the content of the bundle by her feet. I drove up and down streets without direction, trying to think. *What were we going to do? Neither of us had been prepared for this.*

Ninfa was sobbing, and she tried to tell me what had happened back there—about the shock of seeing the perfectly formed little corpse lying on the bare floor in the bathroom.

"He wasn't real to me when he was in my womb,"

she moaned. "Now that I've seen him and held him, I know he was a human being. He was my son."

She clutched her stomach, as if in pain. "I was his mama," she whispered to herself. "He depended on me to give him life...instead, I m-u-r--"

"Shut up!" I didn't let her finish. The word was already etched in my mind—murder! *MURDER!—I was a murderer.* It was our child wrapped in that bundle of rags. Icy terror filled me and I was bathed in a cold sweat. My knuckles whitened around the steering wheel. *What if we were caught with the dead baby!*

We were near Mama's house, and I stopped to find a pick and shovel. No one saw me, and we drove straight to an empty lot. It was late at night, and under cover of darkness, I dug a deep grave. So deep no dog could dig it up.

Ninfa watched, holding the bundle tightly in her arms.

"Put the baby in," I commanded. Quickly I filled in the hole and scattered a few stones over the surface. I felt a wave of relief as we walked away.

In the weeks that followed Ninfa grew silent; she was either loaded on pot, pills, or booze.[n] I was concerned for her. "Slow down, Ninfa. Seems like you wanna self-destruct."

"I can't handle it, Freddie," she broke down and sobbed. "Since we buried our baby, it seems like I'm losing my mind. I was never scared of darkness before; now I can't sleep without a light on. I wake up and hear noises in the night. I'm scared, Freddie. What's happening to me, what do I do?"

I embraced her. "There's nothing to be scared of,

---

[n] booze – alcoholic beverages

Ninfa," I tried to reassure her. "No one saw us, no one's gonna get you. Just don't think about it anymore."

She wept in my arms. Now I could understand why she was staying loaded. She was trying to erase from her memory what we had done to our own flesh and blood. Our secret was hidden, but I wondered...*Would we ever be able to forget?*

To support our increased drug use, I took up shoplifting. I would first go down Guadalupe Street on the west side of town and take orders for merchandise from the barmaids. Women's underwear was easy to steal and sell, and I soon had a regular clientele.

One day I was picking up my "orders" in a department store, carefully selecting the right sizes and colors before stuffing them under my coat. I didn't see the cop who was watching me 'til he came running. Throwing my loot in different directions so he wouldn't catch me with stolen goods, I took off up one aisle and down the next. The officer was faster and soon had me in handcuffs.

"*Pásame quebrada*–Give me a break," I pleaded. "I'm hooked."

"No breaks, you dirty junkie. I've got a job to do!" He pushed me out of the store and into his car.

By the time we arrived at the city jail, I was starting to get sick. "Let me make a phone call, officer," I begged. "I won't make it if I kick in here!"

"Later, junkie," he said harshly, "later."

One of the guards walked me to my cell block. I could hear winos singing Spanish ballads. Some poor guys were coughing so bad it sounded like the T.B. Ward. The cold chills had hit me, and I was trembling, then sweating with hot flashes.

An old junkie-turned-wino shouted at the singers,

"Shut up you guys, can't you see the man's kicking cold turkey!º"

"*Gracias*–Thanks," I barely whispered as the jail door slammed shut behind me.

Finally, I was allowed to call Ninfa. The following morning when I dragged into court, she and Mama were there. "Theft under fifty dollars is a misdemeanor in the state of Texas," I heard the judge warn me, "but you better straighten out." He let me off with a long lecture. Ninfa paid the fine and I was released. Within an hour, I had a needle in my veins.

"Can't go on like this," I groaned. "I hate it; I'm living like an animal. I've got to stop!"

I had heard about the United States Public Health Hospital for Narcotic Addicts in Forth Worth, Texas, and I wanted to go, but Ninfa was pregnant again. This time, she would hear nothing of an abortion.

"Don't worry about us," she urged me. "We'll be all right. You go on and get well."

In the spring, I committed myself to the hospital for six months. I took every therapy they offered, determined not to leave 'til I was cured. Our tiny daughter, Josie, named after my mama, was born while I was in the hospital. She was two months old when I was told that I had successfully completed the psychiatric treatment and was discharged. That evening I arrived in San Antonio and went directly to the pusherᵖ before going home.

"You're high!" Ninfa screamed as I walked into the house.

---

º kicking cold turkey – withdrawing from drugs without medication

ᵖ pusher – person who sells drugs

"How do you expect me to make it, if you don't trust me?" I bluffed.

She said no more, but within days, the familiar pattern of drug addiction gave me away. While Ninfa worked, I was to stay home and watch Josie. Instead, I took the baby along with me on burglaries and when I went to score.

One hot and humid morning, after scoring, I drove to the nearest gas station, took Josie into the men's rest room and put her down on the wet cement floor while I prepared my fix. I was tense and in pain. The sweat ran into my eyes and burned, blurring my vision. Nothing went right. Josie started to cry. Someone banged at the door, wanting to use the rest room. I pierced my arm over and over, missing the vein. I felt like screaming at my four-month-old baby—but just then the needle hit a vein. At once every muscle in my body relaxed.

I felt good, but glancing in the mirror, I saw myself— hollow cheeked and unshaven. I hadn't bathed for several days, and the odor of my own body nauseated me. I bent down to pick up my little girl from her "bed" of dirty toilet paper. The foul stench tore at my nostrils, but she was smiling up at me, her big eyes brimming with tears, her hands reaching up.

"Man! How did I get this low?" I whispered as I held her close. "I never wanted it this way, *mi bebita*.[q]"

The tender moment was soon forgotten. In the *barrio* with my friends, I lost track of time. They took turns holding Josie and feeding her with a spoon from baby-food jars. But when the effect of my fix started to wear off, I panicked and took her to

---

[q] *mi bebita* – my little baby

Mama's.

"It's Alfredo," Papa opened the door for me.

"You're so skinny," Mama touched my arms. "Come in the kitchen; I'll fix you something to eat."

"I don't want food, Mama," I answered. "I'm starting to get sick again."

"Well then, let me at least change Josie's diaper. Look how wet and dirty she is." She took the baby and I slumped on the sofa. Papa put down his beer and got up from his chair to hand me a dollar.

"That's all I got, son," he told me, "but you're welcome to it."

Mama was pinning Josie's diaper. "If I give you some money, Alfredo, will you promise to find a place that can cure you?" Her eyes showed concern.

"You know I've tried, Mama. The best doctors in the field can't help me. 'Once an addict, always an addict!' So forget it."

Mama refused to give in. "Go to Los Angeles and stay with your sisters Estella and María," she pleaded. "Maybe leaving San Antonio will do you good." When Ninfa heard of Mama's plan, she immediately agreed. The two of them finally persuaded me to go.

Later that week I boarded a bus for California. I had fixed just before leaving San Antonio, and we stopped long enough in El Paso for me to buy cough medicine with codeine at the nearest drug store. I was starting to get sick; the codeine would ease some of my withdrawal pain.

At the Los Angeles bus station, my sister Estella was waiting for me. As soon as we got to her house, I took off in search of drugs. By now I was really sick. In downtown Los Angeles I was lucky to bump into Raider, an old drug addict from San Antonio. "Who's got the stuff?" I asked him.

He was "high in the sky" and mumbled, "Two home boys were around a little while ago. Check it out, Freddie, and if you score, you can use my outfit.[r]"

Within the hour, with heroin flowing through my veins, I went back to my sister's house and began unpacking. Once settled, I called Ninfa to join me as soon as possible. In less than a month she arrived in California with baby Josie and found a job as a waitress. We rented a tiny, three-room house a block away from my sister's. She babysat for us while I tried to hold a job, but soon I was back on the streets. Ninfa had to make ends meet on her own.

One evening I got home super stoned,[s] and she confronted me, "You know, Freddie, even your own family says I'm a fool for backing you up. I really thought that my love would be enough to change you; now I know it's not. You haven't changed one single bit, and I'm getting tired."

"We're doing all right," I grumbled. "Quit nagging and leave me alone."

Her eyes flashed in anger. "Do you know what Josie and I ate today? Cheerios—no milk, no sugar—just dry Cheerios! Look around you, Freddie! Days go by when we can't even afford to buy a loaf of bread or a bag of beans, and you dare tell me we're doing all right? ¡Estás loco![t]"

She fought to hold back her tears. "And have you looked at yourself lately? The least little scratch or bump you get develops into big pus pockets. You're

---

[r] outfit – drug injection kit
[s] stoned – to be high on drugs
[t] ¡Estás loco! – You're crazy.

rotting alive and you're doing nothing about it. Man, Freddie, it's not all right!"

I sat down on our small cot and warned her, "Stop your nagging, Ninfa; I'm tired of the whole bit. Just shut up!"

Suddenly I started trembling uncontrollably. My teeth chattered, and I curled up on the cot under our blankets. "Come lie beside me," I pleaded. "I'm freezing."

Touching my forehead Ninfa cried out, "You're burning up with fever, Freddie! Your eyes keep rolling back; you could go into convulsions. You need a doctor!"

"Forget it," I shivered. "Just keep me warm. I'll be all right in the morning."

We had read in the newspapers about addicts dying from heroin accidentally mixed with rat poison, and now, Ninfa was afraid I had become another victim. I really didn't care if I was dying. My life had turned to nothing, and those I loved I had ended up hurting. For a junkie like me there were only three ways out—the penitentiary, the insane asylum, or the city morgue. *If this is poison and it kills me*, I thought, *it'll do me a favor*.

# Chapter 4

# Born Again

Jesus answered and said to him,
"Truly, truly, I say to you,
unless one is born again,
he cannot see the kingdom of God."

John 3:3 (NASB)

Jesus answered, "Truly, truly, I say to you,
unless one is born of water and the Spirit,
he cannot enter into the kingdom of God."

John 3:5 (NASB)

Alfonso and I had both been patients at the Fort
Worth hospital for drug addicts. Now a year and a
half later, I recognized him as he stood on the corner
of Third and Broadway. He was well dressed, so I figured he had to be pushing drugs.

"Freddie," he greeted me as I walked up to him,
"what'cha doing in Los Angeles?"

"I came to kick[a] but you know how it is," I shrugged.
"How about you? Are you holding?[b] I need a fix[c] bad,
man."

He put his arm around me and led me aside. "I got
something better, Freddie—I've got Jesus Christ."

"Yeah, yeah, man," I cut him off, "but have you seen

---

[a] kick – to withdraw from drugs
[b] holding – to have drugs in your possession
[c] fix – an injection of narcotics

anybody with some stuff?[d] I'm sick!"

A big grin broke across his face, "I'm not a junkie no more, Freddie. I haven't used drugs for over a year. Jesus changed my life!"

*I've never seen a cured addict in all my years in the streets*, I thought to myself. *Who's this guy trying to kid?*

Handing me a card, Alfonso looked me in the eyes; his were clear and unwavering. "Put it in your pocket, Freddie. If you ever need help, you can reach me at Teen Challenge."

I stared at him not knowing if he were serious or joking.

"Look, Freddie, if you come to this place, they give you clean sheets and clean clothes every day. While you're kicking, they give you a massage, and after you kick, they'll give you breakfast in bed."

"Pass me a couple more of those cards," I chuckled. "You make it sound like hobo heaven. Maybe some of the guys..." Just then a pusher[e] passed by; I grabbed the cards and ran after him.

After fixing, I went straight home. Comfortable on my cot, I took out the card and read: "Society says, 'Once an addict, always an addict,' but Jesus says, 'I am the way and the truth[1]...and the truth will set you free.'[2]" I turned the card over, and these words stood out, "If you're hooked[f] and need help, call Teen Challenge."

How many times I had attempted to quit drugs and

---

[d] stuff – heroin

[e] pusher – person who sells drugs

[1] John 14:6 (NIV)

[2] John 8:32 (NIV)

[f] hooked – addicted to drugs

had failed. Long ago I'd given up on programs, and now I had no illusions that Alfonso's scheme was any different. But he had offered me a place to crash.

Ninfa was in the kitchen so I raised my voice, "I met this old buddy today."

"So?" she smirked, walking up to where I was lying.

"So-o-o," I repeated, imitating her tone of voice, "he used to be a junkie, but he's not fixing no more. He said that Jesus changed his life, and he gave me this card. He even invited me to go check the place out."

She took the card and threw it back at me. "Go anywhere you want to, just get out of here!" she yelled. "Man, you don't even care if your own daughter sees you inject the needle in your vein. You've lost all self-respect. Do me a favor, Freddie. Call your friend and just leave."

Still not sure of what I really wanted, I walked to the phone booth down the street and made my call. At least I could stay at Teen Challenge for a couple of weeks and get Ninfa off my back.

"Alfonso? This is Freddie. Why don't you come over and pick me up."

"I'll be right there. Where do you live?"

After giving him directions, I waited outside the house for them while Ninfa watched from the doorway. Half an hour later, Alfonso arrived with Amos, one of the program counsellors.

"Are you ready?" Alfonso placed his hand on my shoulder.

I nodded.

"Then get your things."

When I didn't move, Amos thought I'd changed my mind about going. He tried to convince me, "Jesus can really change you, Freddie. He wants to use your life."

I looked down at my dirty, gray T-shirt and filthy, khaki pants; they were all the clothes I owned. I weighed only 128 pounds and had a thirty-inch waist. *If this Jesus really wants to use me*, I thought to myself, *His army must be in bad shape.*

Amos opened his Bible and read out loud: "'For God so loved the world, that He gave His only begotten Son, that whoever believes in Him should not perish, but have eternal life.'[3] That means you, Freddie. God so loved you that He sent Jesus to pay the price for your sins. He died on the cross so you wouldn't have to die a junkie."

I shook my head, "That doesn't make sense, man."

He grinned, "It will, Freddie, it will. Get your things and let's go."

"This is it, man," I tried to hide my embarrassment. "I'm wearing my whole wardrobe."

Ninfa had listened attentively. I knew she was thinking it was another one of my games. When I got into the van, she turned without a word and went inside the house slamming the door behind her.

Alfonso was driving and Amos turned to me, "Got a cigarette, Freddie?"

"Sure," I proudly handed him my new pack.

With a smile, he tossed it out the window.

"*¡Ese!*–Hey! That was a full pack! What's wrong with you guys!"

"You can't smoke at the place we're going," Amos calmly replied.

*Man*, I thought, *I really got myself into it this time.*

---

[3] John 3:16 (NASB)

When we got to the Center, I was surprised to see that it was a two-story home, not an institution. In the hallway Alfonso stopped me, "We're gonna have to frisk you before you're admitted, Freddie."

"Go ahead." By now I was prepared for anything.

Alfonso helped fill in my admittance papers, and I was assigned one of the eight bunks in the attic dorm. There I was greeted by a young Mexican-American who shook my hand.

"Would you care for some coffee? I'm Ralph 'Rah-DREE-gez.'"

"You mean 'Rodríguez,'" I corrected him. "You ashamed of your Spanish name?"

Smiling a little, he asked, "What's your name?"

"Alfredo!" I growled. "Alfredo Francisco García."

"That's Freddie in English, right?" Without waiting for my answer, he added, "Let me ask you, Freddie, do you know Jesus as your Savior?"

*Seguro que sé de Cristo.*[g]

"Huh?" Ralph looked blank. "Would you please speak to me in English? I don't understand Spanish."

"Aren't you a Mexican-American?"

"Yes," he smiled, "but I don't speak Spanish."

"You know what, man," I snarled, "you're a disgrace to the Brown race. You ain't got nothing to say that I want to hear. *¡Descuéntate!*–Beat it! You guys are bad news."

I went to bed that evening worried about getting sick in the middle of the night. To my surprise, I fell asleep almost immediately.

When I woke up the next morning the familiar symptoms of withdrawal had begun, but they were

---

[g] *Seguro que sé de Cristo.* – Sure I know about Christ.

not nearly as bad as I had expected. By my bedside sat a guy named Eddie reading his Bible. "What'cha doing here?" I mumbled.

"I've been praying that Jesus help you make it," he grinned at me. "If you need a rubdown, coffee, prayer, or anything else, I'll more than gladly do it for you, brother."

"Brother?" I sneered. "I ain't your brother, and I don't need your help either. When I kick, I don't want nobody around. Beat it!"

He gave me a friendly smile but didn't leave. For the next six days I was sick, but he didn't leave me alone. Even when I angrily threw the food tray on the floor, Eddie picked up the mess without complaining. He kept coming back with his Bible to see how I was doing and to read to me. When I wouldn't let him near, he knelt by the next bunk to pray for me.

"What's the matter with these *batos*?[h]" I grumbled under my breath. "All they talk about is Jesus... morning, noon, and night."

I was required to attend morning chapel services as soon as I was well enough. The first day, I walked into chapel during prayer time and witnessed a spectacle I'll never forget. The room was packed; Sonny Arguinzoni, the Home supervisor, and about fifty men and women were whooping and hollering, praising Jesus. Some were on their knees and others were standing—all with hands uplifted.

Just to go along with the program, I was about to quietly kneel down, when a coarse, powerful hand forced me to my knees. It was none other than Crazy Carlos, a junkie I'd shot dope with just a couple of

---

[h] *batos* – guys

months back.

"Freddie!" he roared, "I'm gonna pray for you."

He placed his right hand on my forehead and held the back of my head with his left. He jerked my head and yelled in Spanish, "*Señor*–Lord, hit him with a two-by-four. Make Freddie understand, Lord Jesus. Hit him with a sledge hammer!"

I didn't know what to expect. With my head still bowed, I fearfully glanced to both sides. *Did Carlos have someone ready to hit me?* To my relief, nothing happened.

Carlos finally let go of me. I dashed out of chapel determined to leave the program. In the hallway, Louie, one of the counsellors, stopped me. "What's wrong, Freddie?"

"I can't handle all this Holy Roller stuff. I'm splitting."

"Where to?" he challenged me. "You got a better program in mind?"

I stopped cold in my tracks. I hated to admit even to myself, but it was true. I had run out of programs. I couldn't make it an hour out on the streets without drugs... Quietly, I returned to chapel.

Sonny had just introduced a Black man named Andraé Crouch who was sitting at the piano. I had never heard anything like his music. "That dude[i] can really play some heavy sounds," I whispered to the guy next to me.

"That ain't nothing," he told me. "He writes his own songs!"

That evening I asked the fellows in the attic, "Are those guys in chapel for real? And what about Sonny,

---

[i] dude – guy or male

is he putting us on?"

Beto shrugged, "I don't really know; I'm new myself."

"I think it's a religious racket," I declared. "It's all fake and you guys are going for the 'okey-doke.' I believe Sonny is a phony. He was never a junkie; the guy's too clean."

Louie overheard me. "That's not true, Freddie. Sonny was a strung-out[j] junkie in the streets of New York, but he was saved under David Wilkerson's ministry. Sonny was a hard-core addict. If you don't believe me, just sit on the front row the next time he preaches. When he gets excited and swings out his arms, check out his needle scars."

The following morning I was the first man in chapel. The service dragged on 'til Sonny stood up to preach. I didn't care what he had to say, but I had to see if the needle marks were there. When he swung his arms wide open, I leaned forward and stared intently. There they were—the unmistakable tracks left by the continued use of a needle. *Could it be that Louie wasn't putting me on?*

For the next three weeks, I listened to the stories of changed lives, but I didn't feel any different. *Maybe I'm so bad God can't do nothing with me.* The thought made me shiver. *Maybe it's time for me to go back to the streets.*

I often dozed during chapel service because I didn't understand much of what was said. But one morning as Sonny started preaching, he seemed to be talking just to me: "Don't tell me you can't change, that God can't do nothing for you. Every drug addict

---

[j] strung-out – addicted for a long time

knows deep down that he wants to change, but that old, dope-addict pride keeps him from asking Jesus to help him. Pride makes him keep up a big front..."

I was getting more and more uncomfortable. *Some stoolie has been telling on me,* I thought. *Sonny's taking off my covers! He's telling everybody on me.* I wanted to get out of there, but the chapel was packed full and I was sitting in the middle.

Just then, Sonny spread his arms wide, and I couldn't take my eyes off the needle tracks. "Drug addicts like us shouldn't have any pride," he looked straight at me. "The devil has left us filthy and stinking. We've got nothing to be proud of.

"I don't care how much drugs you've shot or how many sins you've committed. Just come forward and ask Jesus to forgive you for all of your sins, and you'll be a drug addict no more. Jesus wants to change your life right now. Just come to Him."

Deep inside I wanted to believe him, but it didn't make sense that someone who died two thousand years ago could help me now. I argued with myself, *I've tried the best hospitals, psychiatrists, psychologists, group therapists, and even curanderas.*[k] *How can Jesus, whom I can't see, feel, or touch, change me?*

Sonny's voice rang in my ears. "Jesus says, 'Behold, I stand at the door and knock; if anyone hears My voice and opens the door, I will come in to him, and will dine with him, and he with Me.'[4]"

He concluded, "Right now, Jesus is knocking at the door of your heart. You're the only one who can open the door and let Him in."

---

[k] *curanderas* – Mexican healers
[4] Revelation 3:20 (NASB)

Andraé was at the piano, and as he struck the first chords of "When He Reached Down His Hand For Me," everyone stood up to sing. The words of the song stirred something deep inside me: "I was near in despair, when He came to me there, and *He showed me that I could be free…*"

My heart was pounding wildly. I wanted to go forward, but I had been the loudmouth who led the rebels in making fun of other guys who went to the altar. *What would they think if I went up there?* There was a battle raging inside me—*What if I go forward and Jesus doesn't change me? I'm just gonna make a fool of myself. The guys will laugh at me.*

I was hoping someone would go first; then I could follow, but the turmoil within drove me. I couldn't wait. I stumbled into the aisle, and with every single step, I felt my pride being stripped away. I didn't care who laughed at me; something stronger than my pride drew me forward.

At the altar, my knees gave way under me. I wanted to speak to God, tell Him how much I hurt, and ask Him to forgive me, but I didn't even know how to pray.

Tears flooded my eyes and a cry of despair rose within me, "*¡Pásame quebrada, Señor!*—Give me a break, Lord! I'm tired of using drugs; I'm tired of the life I've lived. Forgive me for all of my sins and give me a break, Jesus."

I felt a warmth spreading inside me. Somehow I knew it was God's love enclosing my heart, breaking the hard shell around it, releasing all the hurt, bitterness, and hatred I'd harbored for years…washing it all away and setting me free.

My tears flowed until I felt good and clean inside. Even my mind was free from the constant thoughts of the eyedropper and the needle. The desire for drugs was gone!

When at last I got up from the altar of prayer, I knew there was a difference in me. Deep inside there was a certainty; Jesus had forgiven me. He had changed me.

I walked out of chapel and felt like hugging the whole world. Just then an Anglo ex-junkie nicknamed "Rainbow Larry" walked by. Without even thinking, I grabbed him by the arm and gave him a hearty Mexican *abrazo*.[1] Suddenly, it hit me–*I hugged a White guy!* The hostility and hatred I had toward the Anglo was gone!

Wondering what was happening to me, I walked out into the backyard. There was a rose bush by the fence. I stopped and looked at the flowers as if I had never seen them before. Gently, I touched the velvety petals and bent to smell the fragrance. *Why had I never noticed such beauty? What's going on?* I thought. *I feel as if I've never lived–like I've just been born!*

Just then, the back door swung open and Ralph Rodríguez came out. He smiled, and I yelled, "You got a minute?"

"Sure, Freddie."

"Forgive me, Ralph," I blurted out. "I want you to forgive me for the way I treated you when I first came in."

"Praise the Lord! Of course I forgive you."

"Thank you, man," I gave him a bear hug.

He raised his hands and shouted, "Praise Jesus Freddie! Praise Him!"

---

[1] *abrazo* – hug

My own behavior puzzled me. In all my twenty-eight years, I had never asked another person to forgive me. But it sure felt good doing it.

Walking back into the living room, I saw a Mexican-American girl holding hands with her Anglo boyfriend. It was a sight that had never failed to infuriate me, but now the anger was gone.

"Man," I marvelled at God's power, "Jesus not only took away my craving for drugs–He's taken away the hatred that embittered my life all these years! Wow!" I gasped in amazement. "Jesus has really set me free!"

I couldn't wait to share the news with Ninfa.

# Chapter 5

# A New Life

How blessed is the man who does not walk
in the counsel of the wicked,
Nor stand in the path of sinners,
Nor sit in the seat of scoffers!

But his delight is in the law of the Lord,
And in His law he meditates day and night.

And he will be like a tree firmly planted
by streams of water,
Which yields its fruit in its season,
And its leaf does not wither;
And in whatever he does, he prospers.

Psalm 1:1-3 (NASB)

It seemed like the phone rang for an eternity before Ninfa's familiar voice answered, "Hello?"

"I beat the habit, Ninfa!" I hollered. "I'm not a junkie no more; Jesus changed me. The craving for drugs is gone! *¡Ya le gané!*[a]"

"That's good," her voice was cold. She obviously didn't believe me.

"You don't understand, Ninfa," I insisted. "Jesus really changed me. Do you remember when I told you I had no peace 'cause I could never get away from the picture of the eyedropper and needle in my mind?"

"Uh huh, I remember."

"Well, it ain't there no more. I've got the peace of

---

[a] *¡Ya le gané!* – I beat it!

mind I've been looking for all my life!"

Ninfa was still unimpressed, "So, when you coming home?"

"Can't do that," I told her flatly, "'cause we're not married."

"We're not what? What's wrong with you, Freddie?" She was getting impatient. "We've got two kids, remember? What'cha mean you can't come home?"

"I'm gonna follow Jesus," I tried to explain. "I don't want to lose Him. If you wanna come along and live for Jesus too, then I'll marry you. If you don't wanna follow Jesus, then it's good-bye, Ninfa. I'm gonna cut you loose."

She was silent for a long time then calmly replied, "Let me think about it. Call me tomorrow and I'll have an answer for you then."

The instant she hung up, I had a talk with Jesus. "Lord, You know I never wanted to get married again, but I love Ninfa and I don't want to cut her loose. Your Word says I shouldn't marry an unbeliever,[1] so if You want Ninfa to be my wife, reach her, Lord, save her, and change her like You did me—before we're married. Amen."

Next day I called, anxious to know her decision.

"I've wrestled back and forth all night long," she confessed, "but all my reasoning boils down to the simple fact that I love you, Freddie, and I'll do whatever you think is best for us."

"Good," I was glad. "I'll pick you up in about two hours, and we'll go get our blood tests."

Once the fellows at the Center found out I was getting married, Wayne lent me his suit; another guy

---

[1] 2 Corinthians 6:14 (NASB)

gave me a tie, and still another gave me a couple of bucks.

"Wow!" Ninfa exclaimed the minute I walked into our house. "This is the first time I've ever seen you in a suit, Freddie. You look good!"

She tried to hug me, but I held her hands firmly and kissed her lightly on the cheek. "Don't, Ninfa," I pleaded, "we can't be together 'til we're married."

Pulling away from me, she flared in anger, "Who'ya trying to fool? This is Ninfa you're talking to!"

To avoid conflict, I smiled and took her hand. "Come on, let's go or they'll close the doctor's office. I'll explain on the way."

Later I phoned the Center. "Sonny? This is Freddie. We've got our blood tests and license. What do we do now?"

"Wait right there," he told me. "I'll send Bob to pick you up."

When we got to the Center, Sonny called me into his office. "All the fellows are getting ready to go to Pastor Benjamin Crouch's church," he informed me. "I've talked to him already, and he said he'll be more than glad to marry you after the service."

Pastor Crouch had counselled me the week before about my common-law marriage; I was grateful that he would marry us. Somehow everything seemed to be falling in place.

By the time we got to the church, the worship service had already started. "Praise the Lord!" Pastor Crouch greeted me at the door. Putting his hand on my shoulder, he took me aside, "After church, we'll go over to my home, and I'll marry you in a quiet ceremony. Okay?"

"Fine," I agreed. "But, sir, there is one thing; you

know that the girl I plan to marry isn't a Christian."

He nodded.

"I haven't told her this," I cleared my throat, "but if she doesn't surrender her life to Jesus tonight, I'm not going through with the marriage."

"I understand, son," he embraced me with compassion. "I really do."

An usher had already seated Ninfa. Now, I quietly sat down beside her. She was enjoying the music. Silently I prayed that Jesus would touch her. During the sermon, she was attentive, and when the invitation came to accept Christ, Ninfa leaned forward in her seat.

"Are you tired of the life you've lived?" the preacher asked. "Is your load so heavy it's weighing you down? Come to Jesus; He'll carry your load. He'll give you the joy and peace you've been longing for."

Poking me with her elbow, Ninfa whispered urgently, "Freddie, a voice inside me says to go up there, but another voice says, 'Don't go, 'cause then people will know you're a sinner.' What do I do?"

"The desire to go forward comes from the Holy Spirit, and the voice that tells you not to go is Satan," I explained. "Only you can choose which voice to obey."

Without hesitating, Ninfa jumped up from the seat. Her face was wet with tears as she made her way to the crowded altar. My heart beat faster. "Something's happening, Lord," I whispered. "Thank You, Jesus!"

Ninfa stood before the altar; sobs shook her body. I prayed, "Lord, help her, save her." Just then a Black woman stepped beside her and put an arm around Ninfa's shoulders, whispering in her ear. Ninfa raised her hands, and I saw them praying together. The Black woman returned to her seat, and Ninfa remained at the altar in prayer, her hands still uplifted, her face glowing. My heart swelled with gratitude; I knew she had made her peace with God.

Pastor Crouch saw what had happened. He asked Ninfa to remain up by the altar and motioned for me to come stand beside her.

"You all right?" I whispered. "Did you ask Jesus to forgive you for your sins?"

Ninfa nodded, "Yes, Freddie. This Black woman told me to raise my hands towards heaven and ask Jesus to forgive me for all of my sins—and I did it, Freddie," she smiled through tears. "I did it."

Pastor Crouch placed an arm around each of us and turned to the congregation: "Let me tell you, saints, this man and this woman have lived in sin for fi-i-i-ve years. I had planned to marry them quiet-like at my home after the service. But tonight... tonight we have seen Jesus move in their lives, and we're gonna have us a wedding in the House of the Lord instead."

"Amen!" The congregation roared approval, "Amen!"

"But I can't get married in the church," Ninfa whispered frantically. "I've got two kids already."

Pastor Crouch smiled, "The Word of God says, '...the blood of Jesus His Son cleanses us from all sin,' and 'if we confess our sins, He is faithful and righteous to forgive us our sins and to cleanse us from all unrighteousness.'[2] Did you hear that?" he smiled at Ninfa. "Jesus said ALL unrighteousness!"

---

[2] 1 John 1:7,9 (NASB)

"That's right!" several in the congregation called out. "That's Bible!"

Within minutes the ex-drug addict men and women from the Center had started to get organized. They ushered the bride-to-be outside, and I was told to take my place at the altar. Gary, one of the staff workers, quickly volunteered to be Best Man.

Andraé Crouch started playing the "Wedding March" and slowly, down the aisle, came God's choice of groomsmen and bridesmaids—all ex-addicts, transformed by the power of Jesus Christ. Side by side they marched—Anglos, Blacks, and *chicanos*[b]—taking their places at every pew.

As Andraé struck the chords announcing the entrance of the bride, Ninfa appeared escorted by Jack, one of the White guys from the Center. He was to officially give the bride away. Ninfa was wearing a red outfit, her only skirt and a short-sleeve jacket to match. Her shoes were secondhand; we had bought them that afternoon. Her long, dark hair was combed back and pinned in a soft upsweep. Her eyes were puffed and her face streaked with tears, but I had never seen such radiant beauty. Jesus in her life made all the difference.

Quietly she took her place beside me at the altar, and we both faced Pastor Crouch. "Freddie," he looked straight at me, "do you take Ninfa Q. Briseño to be your wife, to have and to hold from this day forward, for better for worse, for richer for poorer, in sickness and in health, to love and to cherish till death do you part?"

---

[b] *chicanos* – a U.S. citizen of Mexican descent born in the United States

My heart was bursting with gratitude and amazement. God had answered my prayer. "I do," I said firmly.

Pastor Crouch turned to Ninfa: "Ninfa, do you take Alfredo Francisco García to be your husband, to have and to hold from this day forward, for better for worse, for richer for poorer, in sickness and in health, to love, honor, and obey till death do you part?"

Ninfa's hand tightened in mine. "I do," she said solemnly.

Beaming with happiness, we went home. Our honeymoon was a new experience; Christ in our lives gave us a deeper love for one another.

Several days later, when my "honeymoon pass" was over, I returned to the Center. I'd been there a few weeks, when one night I was kept awake by the sound of loud praying coming from the second floor.

"They don't have to holler," I grumbled, as I groped my way down the attic stairway. "I'll just ask them to lower their voices. *Se salen estos batos.*[c]"

I opened the door to the dorm, and all irritation faded as I sensed the presence of the Lord. There, between the rows of beds, were "Rainbow Larry," Bobby, John, David, and Beto—jumping and leaping, their hands lifted towards heaven, praising God. Without a second thought I joined them.

Before long, Sonny and fellows from the other dorms had arrived. Soon there were more than twenty-five of us, our voices rising in exuberant praise— some in English, some in Spanish, and some in unknown tongues. In the midst of it all, I also found myself speaking an unknown language that flowed

---

[c] *Se salen estos batos.* – These guys are out of order.

from deep within me, intoxicating me with a new joy.

About two hours later, when things finally settled down, Sonny took those of us who were new converts aside to explain what had happened. "Jesus just baptized you in the Holy Spirit!"[3] he smiled. "The Bible says that 'you shall receive power when the Holy Spirit has come upon you,'[4] power to be a better witness for Jesus. So, don't neglect praying in tongues; do it every day."

Back in my bunk in the attic, I thought about all that had happened. Now I understood what Jesus meant when He said, "He who believes in Me, as the Scripture said, 'From his innermost being shall flow rivers of living water.' But this He spoke of the Spirit, whom those who believed in Him were to receive...."[5]

\*    \*    \*

Less than two weeks later, the position of cook for the Center became available, and Ninfa was offered the job for a small salary plus room and board. Gratefully, we accepted and moved into a small, private room on the second floor.

Ninfa soon learned her way around the kitchen. With each day, she and I drew closer to God and to each other. We were able to attend chapel and Bible studies; we prayed together and shared what we were learning from God's Word. Before I came to Christ, my reading had been limited to comic books, but when Jesus became real in my life, I hungered to know His Word more and more.

[3] John 1:33 (NASB)

[4] Acts 1:8 (NASB)

[5] John 7:38-39 (NASB)

With our first earnings from the Center, I bought a Bible commentary, a dictionary, and a notebook and spent many hours studying at my makeshift desk. Early one morning while Ninfa was cooking breakfast, I walked in and announced: "I feel that Jesus wants me in Bible school."

Her face lit up and she gave me a big hug. "Let's go for it, Freddie! All the time you were on drugs, I stood by you; now that it's for Jesus, I'm with you all the way."

We were still talking, when a tiny voice over the loudspeaker in the kitchen started singing, "Sweet Jesus, Sweet Jesus, what a wonder You are..."

"Listen, Freddie!" Ninfa was excited. "That's our Josie."

Hurrying over to the chapel, we found our three-year-old daughter singing at the microphone as Andraé accompanied her on the piano. I couldn't help but think of the many times I had carried her with me while I burglarized. The memory of it gave me chills. "Jesus," I whispered, "thank You that my family is no longer hurting because I'm a junkie. *Gracias, Jesucristo.*[d]"

With her hand in mine, Ninfa softly repeated, "Thank You, Jesus."

Drug addiction had never left room for anything but drugs. The reality of what I had missed as a father hit me with new force as I watched my daughter singing to Jesus. "I remember reading in the Bible," I told Ninfa, "that 'children are a gift of the Lord.'[6] A gift is something to be enjoyed and appreciated. Now that

---

[d] *Gracias, Jesucristo.* – Thank You, Jesus Christ.

[6] Psalm 127:3 (NASB)

we're Christians, I don't want to miss out on that joy no more!"

Ninfa's eyes were brimming with tears, and I held her close. "Let's ask Jesus to teach us to be good parents, and if it's His will, that He give us another son. I want to enjoy him from day one. I've even thought of naming him Paul."

"It's a beautiful name," she gave me a quick hug and turned to pick up Josie. I joined her, and with my arms around both of them, we prayed.

*       *       *

More and more I yearned to serve God with all my life, and a few months later, I went to see Sonny and his wife, Julie. "I've been thinking about going to the Latin American Bible Institute in La Puente, California," I told them.

"Praise the Lord!" Julie cheered. "We'll help you fill out the application. Right, Sonny?"

"*¡Seguro!*—Sure!" he smiled. "Tell you what, Freddie, I'm looking for a church building 'cause the Lord's called me to pastor. I'd like you to help out in Victory Temple as soon as I get it."

"Wait a minute, Sonny," I stuttered. "I just want to go to school 'cause I got a hunger to learn more about Jesus. I don't know if I have a calling for the ministry."

"Freddie," Sonny declared, "I know you've been called to the ministry 'cause I've seen the way addicts and criminals seek you out. They want your counsel, your opinion, your fellowship. The love of Jesus in your life is the magnet that draws them, and that, Freddie, can only come from God."

I respected Sonny's opinion and didn't argue–but I wondered if God could really use me.

As soon as my application for Bible school was in the mail, I set out to do something I knew I had to do– go back to San Antonio and tell the drug addicts about Jesus. Ninfa and I wrote up the story of how Jesus had freed me from drugs, and we had 10,000 pamphlets printed.

In early spring, I caught a ride to San Antonio with a friend. Ninfa was pregnant and couldn't come with me. Papa and Mama were waiting for me, but I could tell they were not convinced I was really changed. Mama kept glancing at my arms, checking for fresh needle marks.

I took my pamphlets first to several churches, hoping to find volunteers to help me distribute them to the addicts on the streets. No one offered to help, so I sought the Lord in prayer. My old house on 658 N. San Eduardo Street was empty, and I went there to be alone, to cry out my despair, to seek direction. Falling on my knees on the bare floor, I cried, "I know You led me here, Jesus; please help me reach the addicts. They need to hear about Your love for them."

I had the assurance that God was with me. And somehow I felt that He wanted me to go see the pushers[e] I used to know. It didn't make sense. Again I prayed, "Lord, I know it's Your will for me to reach the addicts, but I can't do it alone." My prayers were a mixture of Spanish, English, and tongues, but the more I prevailed in tongues, the stronger the feeling grew that I was supposed to go to the pushers. I could almost hear a voice speaking inside my head: *"Give*

---

[e] pushers – persons who sell drugs

*the pamphlets to the pushers. An addict has to come to the pusher, and every time he does, the pusher can give him your pamphlet."*

It was hard to believe that the thought was coming from the Lord, but it got stronger, and at last–thinking I had nothing to lose–I decided to give it a try. Boogie was the first pusher I visited on the west side of town. As soon as I knocked, he opened the door and greeted me, "Hey, Freddie, come in. I've heard about you getting religion."

He shook my hand and I showed him my pamphlets. "I've got my testimony here on paper, and I wonder if you'd do me a favor?"

*"Seguro*–Sure. How can I help?"

"Would you give one to every junkie who comes to score[f] from you?"

Boogie looked stunned but didn't hesitate. "You know what, Freddie? It's a privilege to help you." Grabbing a hammer and a couple of nails, he gave them to me. "Here, put your story up on the wall so the guys can see it right away when they come in. Leave me a stack on the table too."

I visited every pusher I knew in town, and they all gave me the same response.

Two weeks later I returned to California, grateful to know that every junkie in San Antonio would have a chance to read that Jesus is the answer. It was my prayer that someday God would send me back to my hometown, to work among the addicts.

My application to Bible school had been accepted, and in June, when Ninfa was eight months pregnant, we moved out of Teen Challenge. Beto helped us load

---

[f] score – to obtain anything, usually drugs; to purchase drugs

our things on the pickup truck belonging to the Center. When we were ready to leave, he slipped away and returned with a small bundle and a rolled-up mattress. "Can I go live with you?" he grinned confidently.

Ninfa and I looked at each other, then laughed. "Hop in," I gestured to Beto. *"Vámonos.*[g]*"

A few weeks later, Ninfa gave birth to an eight-pound, twelve-ounce, baby boy. I saw my son minutes after he was born. He looked strong and healthy. "His name is Paul," I reminded Ninfa, "after the apostle who was bold and faithful to preach the gospel no matter what obstacles confronted him. He wasn't a quitter! I hope my Paul will be just as determined to serve the Lord. Besides," I teased her, "next baby we have, you get to name him."

As often as I could, I spent time with my newborn son, always mindful that only because of Jesus, he and Josie had the security of our love.

\*          \*          \*

My first months in Bible school were a struggle. Ninfa had trouble finding work, and we barely had enough money to pay the rent. Many times we collected empty soda-pop bottles in the streets and sold them to buy milk for Paul. In the back of my mind, I wrestled with the possibility of quitting school and going to work.

One day I came home to find Ninfa crying. "Paul's hungry," she sobbed. "I've given him rice water most of the day, but he wants milk."

"Let's pray right now," I replied, "'cause I don't have

---

[g] *Vámonos.* – Let's go.

a single penny in my pocket." We knelt together. "Heavenly Father," I prayed, "I'm Your son and I'm living in an old, converted garage with my wife and children, selling empty bottles to buy my son's milk. Help me, Lord, 'cause I just don't understand. Maybe I got emotional about Bible school and, instead, should be working. Help me, Jesus, I don't know what to do. Amen."

Two hours later there was a knock on my door. Outside stood Pete and Isaac, and in the driveway was a loaded pickup truck. "Freddie," Pete smiled, "the Lord blessed the Teen Challenge Center with a big milk donation. It's more than we can use, and we felt impressed in our hearts to unload some of it here."

They gave us chocolate milk, buttermilk, skim milk, and regular milk, enough for the entire neighborhood. Humbly, I knelt beside my bed, "Lord Jesus, forgive my unbelief. *Perdóname, Señor.*[h]"

In school, I had another struggle. While my classmates were already preaching sermons, I was still tongue-tied, scared to death they might call on me to speak in public. Anytime I even tried, I stuttered, and my mind went blank. When my classmates discovered that I could barely speak in public, they wondered: "Maybe you're out of God's will, Freddie."

Their words pierced my heart and added fuel to my doubt, *Maybe I'm in the wrong place.* All year long I wrestled with myself, *Am I in God's will?* My heart said "Yes," but my mind said "No."

At the end of the first year, when the bell rang and the students filed out of the auditorium to be dismissed for the summer, I stayed behind. Kneeling by

---

[h] *Perdóname, Señor.* – Forgive me, Lord.

my pew, I rested my head on my Bible, hugged it, and wept. "I've asked You to use my life in reaching the addicts in San Antonio, Lord. If You really can't use me, send anyone You want, but please, send them someone. You know I'm not a quitter, Jesus; it's just that I can't teach or preach. You need someone better qualified. I wanna thank You for the privilege of letting me come one year to Bible school, but I think You've got the wrong man. I don't even have the money to come back a second year, but I love You, Lord, and I'm grateful for everything. Amen."

That same week, a group of men from a Methodist church, who ran a half-way house for teenagers coming out of correctional institutions, asked me to share my story. Afterwards, they asked if Ninfa and I would consider being house parents; all they wanted us to do was to live there and tell the kids about Jesus. This was an answer to prayer.

They helped us move into a large house with three bedrooms, wall-to-wall carpeting, and air conditioning. Rent, food, and expense money would be provided for the next two years! Ninfa and I, with Josie and Paul, had a bedroom to ourselves. In the other two rooms were bunk beds. We would have at least six teenagers in the house at all times.

Beto had been reunited with his wife and children and was no longer living with us. Instead there was Manuel Zertuche–"El Pelón"–a skinny, eighteen-year-old weedhead[i] from San Antonio, Texas. "I read your pamphlet, Freddie," he said. "I knew that if Jesus could change you, He could help me get my act together."

---

[i] weedhead – marijuana user

Manuel stayed but wasn't ready to commit his life to Jesus all the way yet. Many nights we stayed up pleading with him not to go back to the streets. But one morning he was gone. There was a note with the house key on the kitchen table: "I'm sorry, Freddie. I'm going back home. I'm too young to follow Jesus; I still want to have fun."

Ninfa was crying but I told her, "You can't force anyone to love Jesus. All we can do is pray. Maybe one day Jesus will send us back to San Antonio, and we can look him up."

In my third year of Bible school, I still hadn't preached my first sermon, but one morning as I scanned the list of student preachers for the next semester, my heart jumped. There it was in bold letters: FREDDIE GARCIA.

For the next several weeks, I fasted, prayed in tongues,[7] and spent sleepless nights pleading with God. At last I had my sermon outlined. I rehearsed before Ninfa, over and over again. But on the big day, I was still scared. As I stepped to the pulpit, I prayed under my breath, "Help me, Jesus, don't let me make a fool of myself. I don't want to dishonor Your name."

With my outline before me, I launched out and felt suddenly calm. I was not speaking on my own authority but on the authority given me by God. When it was over, my fear returned. "I hope I didn't dishonor You, Jesus," I whispered as my classmates crowded around me.

"You did good, Freddie," they kept saying. "You did very good."

God had helped me and I knew it. I was still terrified of speaking publicly, but if He could use me, I

---

[7] Acts 2:4 (NASB)

would do it.

\*     \*     \*

On graduation day in June, 1970, as I walked across the stage in my cap and gown, I glanced toward the audience. Ninfa sat on the edge of her seat, with Paul and Josie close beside her. Next to them was my mama. She had flown in from San Antonio for this, my special day.

Time had painted Mama's hair with streaks of gray, but her face glowed with happiness as she looked up at me. "Thank You, Heavenly Father," I whispered, "for allowing my mama to see my new life in Christ."

The principal smiled as he shook my hand. With my diploma, I returned to my seat. Gratitude swelled in me: "Lord Jesus, You picked me up out of the gutter; from the very gates of a living hell, You rescued me. All I am and ever will be, I owe to You. All the praise, all the honor, and all the glory is Yours and Yours alone, now and forevermore."

# Chapter 6

# San Antonio, Texas

But you will receive power
when the Holy Spirit comes on you;
and you will be my witnesses
in Jerusalem, and in all Judea and Samaria,
and to the ends of the earth.

Acts 1:8 (NIV)

Three days after graduation, Mama, Ninfa, the kids, and I were on our way back to San Antonio. The days were hot and humid, and the road seemed endless and dreary as our heavily packed, secondhand station wagon chugged along on Interstate 10.

Three-year-old Paul slept in Ninfa's arms in the front seat. Sweat pearled on his forehead and ran into his already moist hair. Mama and Josie were crowded in the back seat, surrounded by boxes and bundles, but no discomfort could quench the happiness in our hearts.

Up ahead was a rest area with tables and benches under huge shade trees. "Look, Daddy!" Josie yelled in my ear, "a place to sit down and eat!"

Turning to Mama in the back seat, Ninfa asked, "What do you think?"

Mama smiled and hinted, "It's past twelve."

I wanted to keep going but was out voted; I pulled the car over. Quickly, Mama and Ninfa put our meal of homemade *tacos*[a] on the picnic table. As soon as we

---

[a] *tacos* – flour tortillas with various fillings

had eaten, I pressed them, "Let's go. We've got a long drive ahead of us."

"What's the hurry?" Ninfa teased.

"I can hardly wait to get to San Antonio," I laughed. "I feel like a wild stallion who's just been turned loose. I'm anxious to taste the victory of reaching the junkies in my hometown for Christ!"

The second day, in the afternoon, we finally reached the Alamo City and drove down the familiar street leading home. With my diploma and graduation picture in hand, ready to show Papa, I walked in. He was seated in his favorite chair facing the door. He looked old, his hair completely white. Mama had told me that his vision was nearly gone. "Papa!" I called out.

"*¿Quién eres?*–Who are you?" He tried to focus his eyes on me.

"I'm your son Alfredo, Papa," I embraced him. "I've just graduated from Bible school–I'm a preacher."

Papa chuckled in disbelief. "Don't lie to me, Alfredo."

"It's true," Mama proudly affirmed. "I saw him graduate."

Papa was silent for a moment, then asked, "Is it true, Alfredo?"

"Yes, Papa," I assured him. "*Soy predicador.*[b] Your son Alfredo is really a preacher!"

Without speaking, Papa slowly got up from his chair and turned to walk towards his room. Scratching his head he murmured to himself, "A preacher?" He shook his head and quietly closed the door behind him.

Mama and I looked at each other. "He can't believe

---

[b] *Soy predicador.* – I'm a preacher.

it," she smiled.

"I don't blame him," I nodded, "not after the life he saw me live before I came to Christ."

We were all exhausted from the trip and went to sleep early, but the next morning the familiar smell of freshly brewed coffee and *tortillas*[c] got me up. Waiting for me in the kitchen with a plate of scrambled eggs and *tortillas* was Mama. "Sit down, Alfredo, I want to talk to you."

Sipping her coffee, she sat down to face me. "When you were hooked[d] on heroin and couldn't make the payments on your house on San Eduardo Street, you know I had to rent it out. Careless tenants have damaged it, but it's still yours."

"Thank you, Mama," I hugged her, "thank you for taking care of my house, but most of all–for believing in me all these years."

Later that morning, Ninfa, the kids, and I got in the car and drove to 658 N. San Eduardo Street. Mama had not exaggerated; the tiny house was in sad disrepair. The outside paint was peeling off, windows were broken, part of the floor was missing, and patches of the ceiling were falling down. Water dripped from both kitchen and bathroom sinks, and the walls were green with moss. The odor of rotting wood and mildew was strong, but even that didn't discourage us.

A few days of scrubbing, cleaning, and emergency repairs did wonders. We moved in and thanked the Lord for our tiny home. It was furnished with the bare essentials, collected for us by Mama: a bed, a

---

[c] *tortilla* – a thin, unleavened pancake characteristic of Mexican cookery

[d] hooked – addicted to drugs

table, a beat-up old sofa, and some chairs and dishes. Our first day there, Mama showed up with my sister Santos. "Alfredo," she called me outside, "look what we got you."

I came out just in time to help them bring in four bags of groceries. There was a twinkle in Mama's eyes I hadn't seen in years. She was happy for us and it showed. A bag of bright red apples caught Paul's attention. Cautiously, he drew closer to Mama watching her every move. She smiled at him, "What do you want?"

"An apple," he shyly replied.

Mama chuckled. "*Pero ¿cómo se dice* apple *en Español*, Paul?–How do you say 'apple' in Spanish?"

My face flushed with embarrassment as my son shrugged his shoulders, "I don't know."

Always Mama had insisted that we speak to her in Spanish. Now she was repeating the familiar challenge to the second generation–her grandchildren. Taking an apple out of the bag, she held it out to him and slowly pronounced, "*Man...za...na*. Say, '*Quiero una manzana*'–I want an apple."

Timidly, Paul repeated after her, "*Quiero...una... manzana*."

"Good," Mama hugged him.

Paul left the room happily munching on his apple. "He does understand Spanish," I apologized to Mama, "and I do remind him to speak it, but most of the children his age speak nothing but English." Mama said nothing but her eyes held a mild reprimand.

Later in the evening I discussed the incident with Ninfa. "All this time I've assumed that Paul would learn to speak Spanish just because we speak it at home, but I was wrong. It doesn't happen automatically; we're gonna have to make time to teach our children. It's not their fault if they haven't learned—it's ours. Let's make sure Josie and Paul practice both their English and Spanish well."

\*         \*         \*

That Saturday, Ninfa and I found ourselves with an added blessing; Frankie, Ricky, and Sandra came to spend the weekend with us. "You've grown so much since the last time I saw you, Frankie!" I wrestled playfully with him on the floor.

"I'm thirteen already, Papa," he boasted.

"He's lying, Dad," Sandra protested. "He won't be thirteen 'til September."

Drawing Ricky to me, I asked, "How old are you, son?" He looked down without speaking and shyly pulled away.

"He's eleven, Dad," Sandra volunteered, "and I'm gonna be nine."

Not 'til the next morning did Ricky feel secure enough to laugh and play while I was watching. "He doesn't know me," I told Ninfa. "I've been away too long. I have to build a relationship with my kids all over again."

When they were ready to leave, Ninfa and I put our arms around them. "Father, in Jesus' name," I prayed, "reach all my children so that they may come to know You as their Lord and Savior."

A few days later, Mama phoned. Her voice betrayed her anxiety. "Papa's ill. Can you help me take him to the doctor?"

After days of testing, Papa underwent surgery to

replace a portion of his abdominal aorta. He was seventy-five years old and the surgeon gave him a fifty-fifty chance of survival. Papa spent seven hours on the operating table while the entire family waited with Mama at the hospital. My brothers and sisters, their mates, their children, and their grandchildren—more than twenty-five of us—were there in the waiting room and corridors, outside the Intensive Care Unit.

An Anglo nurse kindly suggested that we all go home and get some rest, assuring us that the patient was in good hands and there was nothing we could really do for him. No one moved. She was annoyed, so I hastened to explain, "Among Mexican-Americans it is customary for all the family to be present in a situation like this."

"You people don't seem to understand," she was getting agitated. "This man is ill; he mustn't be disturbed. If you all don't leave, I'll have to call the security guard.

"By the way," she added, "when your father leaves the hospital, he's going to need a lot of extra care. You should consider placing him in a convalescent home. Your mother won't be able to take care of him properly, even if she wants to. That's too much stress on a lady her age."

"What did she say, Alfredo?" Mama touched my arm.

"That Papa's better off in a convalescent home."

Mama shook her head and looked at me. I could see fear in her eyes. "Promise me you won't let them put him in a nursing home," she pleaded.

I put my arms around her, "Don't worry, Mama, Papa's coming home. We'll all help take care of him."

When Papa finally came home, the family pitched in financially so that my niece Linda could stay with Mama and help care for Papa full-time. The rest of us took turns coming by daily to check on their needs and help with special chores.

\*　　　　\*　　　　\*

We had been in San Antonio almost two months when I went to visit my old *barrio*.[e] I invited Tony, a Christian friend, to come along. "We're gonna go to the drug connections," I told him. "Bring your guitar and sing to them about Jesus; then I'll witness and preach." I had hoped to see my old friends from the gang but discovered that most of them were doing time in the penitentiary.

Every day Ninfa and I went back to the streets to talk about Jesus. We armed ourselves with pamphlets and walked up one side of the street and down the other. We stopped any White, Black, or Brown junkie who would listen. Most of them were courteous and attentive, but that was all—no response, nothing! Days turned into weeks, and weeks into months without a single addict coming to Christ.

I wasn't having much result in reaching the community with my plea for help to halt the wave of drug addiction either. I had only been able to get a few invitations to speak in schools and civic clubs. "Why aren't things working out?" I wondered out loud to Ninfa. "The junkies I've talked to are still hooked; I'm not reaching them."

"God sees what you're doing," she reminded me.

---

[e] *barrio* – neighborhood

"Look at it this way. You're the first ex-addict in this city allowed to lecture on drug prevention and education in the schools. You're reaching young people before they ruin their lives!

"On the streets, you're not only telling addicts what Jesus can do, you're a living example! You're doing your best, Freddie, and that's all God asks from you."

"That still doesn't solve my problem," I argued.

"Well then," she looked concerned, "are you sure this is where God wants us? Remember, Sonny said he needed you back in Los Angeles."

"I know this is where the Lord wants me," I assured her. "That's not even what I've been talking about! I just can't understand why things aren't working out."

I took off for the streets with a bundle of pamphlets, and when I returned, Ninfa was visibly troubled.

"What's the matter?" I asked.

"Josie came from school crying," Ninfa told me. "She says she hates her dark hair and brown eyes because it makes her look ugly. She wants to have blonde hair and blue eyes."

"Where did she get that from?" I exclaimed.

"She's been hearing again and again how pretty a certain blonde, blue-eyed, little girl at school is," Ninfa replied. "So Josie figured that since she's got brown hair and eyes, she must not be pretty."

Here was a ghost from my own childhood rising to haunt our daughter. "Jesus," I prayed out loud, "I'll never be able to shield my children from the prejudice and inequality that will always be part of this world.

Help us make our daughter understand that You created her to Your glory. Amen."

"Isn't she too small to understand?" Ninfa wondered.

"If she's old enough to see the difference between Brown and White," I replied, "she's old enough to know."

Calling Josie in from her play, I lifted her up on my lap. I stroked her hair, "Do you know that your mama and I love your brown hair?"

"I don't like it," she protested. "I want blonde hair so I can be pretty."

"Tell me," I asked her, "do you know Jesus loves you?"

"Yep," she nodded.

"So guess who picked the color of your hair and your eyes?"

She looked up at me expectantly. I smiled at her, "Jesus did. Let me show you in the Bible." I read, "'...the Lord Himself is God; it is He who has made us, and not we ourselves.'[1] That means, Josie, that when you were in Mommy's tummy, Jesus made every part of you." When I touched her ears, her nose, and her lips, she giggled. "Tell me, Josie, do you like the voice He gave you to sing with?"

She nodded.

"Well," I kissed her, "let's you and me pray and ask Jesus to help you to like the color of your hair and eyes because He picked them out especially for you." We prayed, and a smile brightened her thin face. She threw her arms around my neck and hugged me, then ran out to play.

---

[1] Psalm 100:3 (NASB)

That night I stayed awake. "I know You want me to reach the addicts, Lord, but You also made me a father and gave me the responsibility for a family. Help me to teach my children to love You and to know that You love them."

*       *       *

The city of San Antonio was becoming aware of our presence. I was asked to be on several television panel discussions on drug abuse, and newspapers reported on my lectures in the schools. Wherever I spoke, I told them about Jesus.

A healed drug addict was something of a curiosity, and soon more civic clubs and churches invited me as a speaker. I felt confident that when the right time came, they would help support an outreach to the addicts.

*       *       *

Ninfa and I felt an urgent need to open a Home where addicts could stay. "Talking to them on the streets is not enough," I told her. "We need seven to eight acres of land with at least a six-bedroom home to house them."

We were convinced that once the right property was found, God would give us the money to buy it. Realtors were helpful and we drove all over San Antonio looking at houses. They were either too small or too expensive, too close to town or too far away.

"Where is it, Lord?" I cried. "How long do I have to search?"

In the back of my mind was a persistent thought: *"Open up your home; bring them in to live with you."*

"That can't be God," I argued with myself. "This house isn't fit; it's hardly big enough for a couple with two small children. The roof leaks so bad we have to put two or three buckets in each room when it rains, and we cover ourselves in bed with plastic to keep from getting wet during the night. When it's cold, we stuff newspapers in the cracks of the wall to keep the wind from blowing through."

Common sense told me I couldn't start a Home for addicts, much less a full-scale ministry, in a tiny, run-down place like this. But I couldn't shake off the idea. For days I went to bed thinking about it, and it was my first thought when I woke up.

Ninfa was not aware of my inward battle, but one morning over coffee she suggested, "Freddie, why don't we open up our home and bring the addicts in?"

"Are you out of your mind?" I exploded. "Where would you put them?"

Ninfa's eyes were bright with laughter, "In the daytime, it's no problem." Grabbing the back of her own shirt collar, she giggled, "And at night, we could put hooks on the wall and hang them up to sleep!"

"I don't find that funny!" I stormed out of the house. "Now I really know that can't be from God," I muttered under my breath and headed for the streets.

On Guadalupe Street, Spanish *polcas*[f] were blaring from the juke boxes. Pushers[g] and prostitutes were peddling their wares on the corners, and junkies and winos were crowding the sidewalks. Others were dozing against the buildings. Suddenly my eyes flooded with tears. "Winter is just around the corner,

[f] *polcas* – polkas

[g] pushers – persons who sell drugs

Lord, and they have nowhere to go. Nobody wants them, nobody cares..."

Finally I realized it had been the Holy Spirit convicting my heart all along. "I'll do it, Jesus! You know that my house is too small, but they can come home to live with us."

That night Ninfa and I put our hands on the walls of our home at 658 N. San Eduardo Street, anointed it with oil, and dedicated it to the work of the Lord. We sensed in the air the feeling of excitement. We could almost hear the footsteps of many addicts coming home.

# Chapter 7

# The Wild Bunch

But God has chosen the foolish things of the world
to shame the wise,
and God has chosen the weak things of the world
to shame the things which are strong,
and the base things of the world and the despised,
God has chosen, the things that are not,
that He might nullify the things that are,
that no man should boast before God.

1 Corinthians 1:27-29 (NASB)

A whistle, followed by a pounding on the door, startled me from the supper table.

"Hey, Freddie!" cried a voice.

February's cold and windy evenings darkened early. I pulled the curtain aside and peeked out the window, "¿Quién es?–Who is it?"

"It's me–Joe Zertuche."

When I opened the door, he stumbled inside. The khaki pants and tattered jacket hung loosely on his tall frame, making him look wasted and older than his twenty-one years. "I'm hooked[a] bad, Freddie," he was uptight and shaky. "I'm using heroin every day, and I came to see if you'd let me kick[b] in your home."

"Sure, Joe," I closed the door behind him. "You came to the right place. Jesus can help you kick."

"Man, you don't understand," he shivered. "I'm

---

[a] hooked – addicted to drugs

[b] kick – to withdraw from drugs

gonna get sick! Look at me; I'm getting cold chills already!"

"I understand, Joe." I pulled up my sleeve and pointed to my own needle scars. "But I also know that Jesus has the power to give you victory over your drug addiction." Ninfa and I prayed, and we felt the presence of the Holy Spirit come into the room. Joe breathed deeply and calmed down.

After a week, his physical withdrawal from heroin was complete, and I started teaching him from the Bible. "Drugs ain't never been your problem, Joe. Sin is your problem. It says here in the Bible, 'For all have sinned and fall short of the glory of God.'[1]

"Jesus teaches that '...everyone who commits sin is the slave of sin.'[2] You're a drug addict because you're a slave of sin. But there's hope. Look what the Word of God says: 'If we confess our sins, He is faithful and righteous to forgive us our sins and to cleanse us from all unrighteousness.'[3]

"That means, Joe, that Jesus has the power to break the shackles of sin. He will forgive you and set you free; all you have to do is ask Him. Repent of your sins and you'll be a drug addict no more."

Joe listened attentively but said nothing.

A few days after his arrival, two more hard-core addicts came looking for a place to kick. With three guys added to our family, we had to have more room. We decided to tear down the wall between our tiny kitchen and screened porch in back, enclose the porch and partition off a small bunk room. When I

[1] Romans 3:23 (NASB)

[2] John 8:34 (NASB)

[3] 1 John 1:9 (NASB)

mentioned the plan to the fellows, Joe blurted out, "My brother, Manuel Zertuche–'El Pelón'–knows about carpentry, Freddie, but he's hooked."

"Hooked?" I was surprised. "On heroin?"

"Yeah, Freddie," Joe replied, "he's strung out[c] bad."

"Let's see if he wants to help fix up the place," I urged. "Maybe while he's working here, he'll get a hold of Jesus this time."

That evening Ninfa and I prayed: "Lord, You know how we pleaded with Manuel to surrender to You when he was in California. Touch his heart, Lord. Bring him back to You."

Manuel came by a few days later to see what I wanted repaired. I hardly recognized him; he was only a year older than Joe, but in far worse shape. His long hair was a filthy mass of tangled knots, and through the torn sleeves of his thin shirt, I could see the pus pockets from dirty needles.

My heart went out to him. "You already know about Jesus, Manuel," I put my arm around him. "I don't have to tell you. When you're tired enough and ready to change, ask Him to forgive you for all your sins. He'll set you free from drug addiction."

He hung his head. "I know that I've got to make a choice someday, Freddie," he admitted. "Just keep it cool, okay?"

"Listen to Freddie!" Joe yelled at him. "I accepted Jesus a few days ago. I'm clean. Man, Jesus is all right!"

Manuel ignored his brother and changed the subject. "About this job here, Freddie, can I start now, work late, and spend the night?"

---

[c] strung out – addicted for a long time

"Sure can," I agreed, "just let us pray for you."

"Okay," he bowed his head.

"Lord Jesus, thank You for bringing Manuel; help him make it back to You," we prayed.

The next morning Manuel burst into the kitchen: "Freddie! Ninfa! I asked Jesus to forgive me for all of my sins last night! I told Him how tired I was of being all messed up, and I promised to follow Him no matter what!" He stopped abruptly with a look of pure astonishment: "I'm not sick!" He rubbed his arms. "Maybe I was fixing[d] a poor grade of heroin. That's it, huh, Freddie? Ain't it?"

"No, *bato*.[e]" I corrected him. "That's not it. You're experiencing the healing power of God in your life."

"Thank You, Jesus," Manuel whispered as tears made their way down his face. "Thank You, Jesus."

\*        \*        \*

A local newspaper ran the story of how Jesus was changing the drug addicts on the west side of town. The article drew in four more hard-core addicts.

"What do we do, Freddie?" Ninfa looked around in our crowded living room that served as a dining room and chapel as well. "We've got eight guys living with us already, and three more just called wanting to come in. Where will they sleep?"

"No problem," I said, "just make more room."

I turned to Manuel Zertuche. "Get Joe and the rest of the guys; tell them to help you put out the sofa, the chest of drawers—everything that's in the living room."

---

[d] fix – an injection of narcotics

[e] *bato* – guy

"Put them where?" he grinned.

"Outside!" I pointed to the front yard.

Someone had given us a worn-out piece of canvas. With it, we rigged up a makeshift awning attached to the roof overhang in front. There we stored our furniture. Now we could put the newcomers on the living-room floor.

With eleven guys living with us, there was another problem, and I took it up with the fellows one morning after Bible study. "Ninfa is doing the cooking and washing for all of us. She could use some help with the other chores, so we're all gonna pitch in," I told them. "Each man will be assigned a job for a month; then we will rotate the assignments. Joe, you get the morning dishes; Manuel, you sweep and mop; Lupe, you take the bathroom; Venado, the front yard..."

Excited about what the Lord was doing, I phoned Pastor Sonny back in Los Angeles. "How would you like to see a Victory Home here in San Antonio?" I asked him.

"*¡Bendito sea Dios!*—Blessed be the Lord, Freddie!" he hollered over the phone. "We were just talking about how we can start new ministries in other places. Wait 'til I tell the guys what you're gonna do." He paused for a moment, then added, "This has to be God, Freddie! You go ahead; let the Lord lead you."

"Sonny," it was my turn to pause, "it's already started. We've got eleven guys living with us. Jesus is reaching the addicts of San Antonio, Texas!"

"Praise the Lord!" Sonny rejoiced. "That's the confirmation that you're doing what God called you to do."

\*　　　　\*　　　　\*

Each week, Mama and my sister Santos faithfully brought several bags of groceries. But after a few days, our cupboards were usually empty. "You all know that we've started many a day with no food in the house," I reminded the guys. "But you've also seen that the Lord has answered our prayers, morning, noon, and night, and never let us go without a meal yet."

"Amen!" They jumped up and down and cheered. "Amen!"

"It's true that our menu is beans, rice, or potatoes for breakfast, lunch, and dinner," I grinned. "But I believe that if we ask the Lord to give us some meat, He might just do that. Amen?"

The guys applauded wildly and whistled approval. My friend Tony, who was often there with his guitar, singing with us, laughed. He added, "Every time I eat with you guys, I've had to pray, 'Lord, let these beans taste like meat!'"

His remark set off a new wave of cheering and laughter. Finally our guys calmed down and fell to their knees. In child-like faith, we all began to pray—in English, Spanish, and other tongues.[4] The room resounded with our voices rising in crescendo, then falling to a hush as the gentle presence of the Holy Spirit filled us with awe. Several fellows began weeping; others were caught up in worship, "I love You, Jesus, I love You."

I didn't want to leave, but I had a speaking engagement in one of the schools. When I got home later that afternoon, Roy, one of the newer guys, greeted me excitedly. "The Lord answered our prayers; He sent

---

[4] Acts 2:4 (NASB)

us some meat! A car came by and accidentally hit one of our neighbors' chickens in front of our house! We ran outside, Freddie, and seeing that the chicken was dead, we thanked the Lord, brought it in, cleaned it, and cooked it."

I didn't know whether to get angry or start laughing out loud. My eye caught Ninfa's. "I wasn't here!" she threw up her hands and giggled. "By the time I came home, they'd eaten it up!"

The following day, I went to speak to inmates in the county jail and came home to find a car parked in the driveway. In the house was Benny, my old gang-mate from the *barrio*,[f] putting two heavy bags of groceries on our kitchen table. I knew Benny had recently been released from prison and was back on the streets pushing drugs. He pulled a large money roll from his pocket and handed me three twenty-dollar bills. "Here, Freddie, you don't have to go hungry as long as we're around."

I was moved by his kindness. But I knew it was not his money; it belonged to his supplier. I closed his hand around the bills, "Don't, Benny, you'll come out short when you report to the 'main man.'"

Benny grinned and slurred, "Don't worry, Freddie, I've been short before." He pressed the bills into my hand. "You need them to feed these guys."

He headed for the door and stopped, "I'm really glad you're making it, Freddie. You're clean, man, and that's what really counts. Keep it up."

"*Muchas gracias*–Thanks a lot, Benny," I shook his hand. "You know that Jesus can change you, too."

He looked down. "That's not for me, Freddie; I'm not

---

[f] *barrio* – neighborhood

ready yet." He glanced at his watch, "I've got to split. *Ai te miro.*[g]"

When he was gone, Ninfa told me that Benny had been by the house earlier, looking for me. He had opened the refrigerator hunting for something to munch on, and when he saw it was empty, he left. Ninfa's eyes filled with tears, "He's strung out, Freddie; still, he took time to go buy us some food."

That same week, a light-blue station wagon pulled up early in the morning. Out stepped a man wearing a clerical collar. He introduced himself as Father Renfro, one of the priests of Our Lady of Guadalupe Catholic Church. He smiled, "I read about your work in the newspaper. I don't know what I can do to help, but I brought you a few groceries, and here is a twenty-five dollar monthly pledge from our church."

As if on cue, people from the community started bringing food, clothing, and small donations of money. I saw our guys' faith increase as they experienced such tangible answers to prayer.

"This is what the Bible talks about," I explained during chapel service. "Jesus says, 'But seek first His Kingdom and His righteousness; and all these things shall be added to you.'[5]

"You're gonna see Jesus do the same all over Texas. There'll be Victory Homes like this one in all the major cities, reaching out to those who are hurting, and you're gonna see Jesus answer their prayers too!

"I'm gonna tell you something else," I continued. "God is training you right now, 'cause He's gonna use you guys to pioneer those ministries."

---

[g] *Ai te miro.* – I'll be seeing you.
[5] Matthew 6:33 (NASB)

"But, Freddie," Manuel Zertuche looked worried, "I don't even know how to talk to anyone about Jesus."

"How did you learn to drive a car?" I grinned. "You watched somebody do it and you learned, right?"

Manuel nodded.

"Well, I'm gonna teach you how to witness for Jesus," I moved my chair out of the way. "We'll start right now. You pretend that you're a guy walking up the street, and I'm the Christian who's gonna witness to you. Watch how I do it, and then we switch— you witness to me."

Manuel jumped from his seat, and the rest of the guys cheered and kicked back to watch the scene.

"Pay close attention," I told them, "'cause after Manuel, you're each gonna do it." Over and over we repeated the scene 'til everyone had taken a turn. "Now you've got it," I was proud of them. "Let's pray for thirty minutes. Then we hit Guadalupe Street."

Out on the sidewalk, I gave each a handful of pamphlets, "I'll talk to the first guy who comes along. Watch me; then you do it." We didn't leave the street 'til every one of our guys had their chance to witness about Jesus.

They returned home excited, each with a story to tell. "I was nervous, *bato*," Lupe confessed, "but then I prayed, and Jesus gave me the right words to say."

"That same thing happened to me!" Roy yelled.

"Amen! Me too!" They looked at each other in amazement. "Hallelujah! Thank You, Jesus!" Our small living room was filled with the sound of praise. The fellows were clapping their hands and stomping their feet; they whistled, hollered, and sang at the top of their voices, "Thank You, Jesus!"

Just then there was a knock on the door. Ninfa

opened it. A police officer stood outside looking concerned, "Ma'am, we got a disturbance call that there was a fight going on."

Ninfa smiled, "No one's fighting, officer. We're just praying, singing, and praising God. You can come in and take a look."

The officer smiled, "You go ahead and keep doing what you're doing. We just came to comply with the call." He turned around and left. We stopped our worship long enough to have supper, then spent the evening in Bible study.

\*　　　\*　　　\*

During one of our late evening prayer times, a frightening chill spread through the room. We heard a thud, and I felt something crawling past my feet. It was Roberto, one of our newcomers, wiggling on his back across the floor towards the front door. His eyes were closed, and his tongue flickered, snake-like, in and out. He pushed his head against the screen door, tearing it, and I was jolted into action. "Help me stop him," I told the guys. "He might hurt himself."

We pulled him by the legs back into the room, and the guys, figuring he was sick, laid hands on him and started praying. Immediately Roberto hissed, spat, and bit the Bible closest to him. Then he spoke in a strange, deep voice, "My name is Satan."

Ernie, trembling with fear, asked, "Freddie, can the devil really possess a person?"

"Yes he can, if the person isn't saved,[6]" I explained. "But he can't possess a born-again[7] Christian,

---

[6] Acts 16:31 (NASB)

[7] John 3:3,5 (NASB)

washed in the blood of the Lamb,[8]" I assured him.

Roberto had fallen asleep and we all went to bed.

"Freddie," Ninfa woke me the next day, "have you seen my Bible?"

"No, but you can borrow mine." I had put it on the shelf by our bed the night before. Now it was gone. I started to get up and stepped on someone. "What's going on!" I jumped back into bed.

Joe and Roy had silently crept into our room during the night and were asleep on the floor by our bed. A bit sheepishly they explained, "We were scared to sleep near Roberto."

"Get up," I laughed. "Help us find our Bibles."

"Ours are gone too!" guys were calling out from all over the house.

"Look, Freddie!" Ninfa burst out laughing. She pointed to Ernie's bed in the kitchen, "He's got all our Bibles!"

Ernie was still asleep, surrounded by open Bibles, but awoke when we all gathered around his bed. He, too, confessed he'd been afraid.

I picked up my Bible. "It says here that '...greater is He who is in you than he who is in the world,'[9]" I declared. "There's nothing to be afraid of as long as Jesus is Lord of your life."

"Freddie, why isn't Roberto set free?" Manuel Zertuche asked.

"Jesus teaches us that this kind of demon 'does not go out except by prayer and fasting,'[10]" I explained.

"Then, let's all fast," the guys agreed.

---

[8] Revelation 7:14 (NASB)

[9] 1 John 4:4 (NASB)

[10] Matthew 17:21 (NASB)

But Roberto slipped away that very day. The guys were discouraged, and I told them, "The best thing we can do for Roberto is pray that one day he will let Jesus set him free."

*   *   *

I'd been out trying to solicit funds to help me feed our boys, and I came home to find a young man seated on the front steps waiting for me.

"This is Juan Garza," Ninfa introduced him. "He needs a place to kick."

"Man, I've got a full house already," I shook my head. "It's not that I don't want you, but there are guys sleeping all over the floor. I have no more room."

"Sir, I'm willing to sleep anywhere," he politely insisted. "I just want to kick, Mr. García."

"Well," I opened the door, "if you don't mind, we won't either. Come on in!"

He arrived just in time to join our weekly rap session. Joe spoke up first, "I don't have nothing to gripe about the program rules. It's just a problem with me." He looked awkward, "Don't laugh, man, but just now, Freddie, you introduced me to the new guy as Joe Zertuche, right?"

"That's your name isn't it?" I chuckled.

"That's the point, man!" He was upset. "I don't like my last name. You don't have to say Zertuche; just say, 'This is Joe.'"

"What's wrong with your last name?" Ninfa asked. "I think it's beautiful."

"*¡No me cae!*—I don't like it!" he yelled.

*Here we go again, Lord*, I silently prayed, *another Mexican-American who doesn't like his Spanish name.*

*It's different people at different times but the same problem. Give me wisdom to help him understand.*

"It's wrong to put yourself down because of your name or your race," I told Joe. "That's self-hate. In God's eyes, it doesn't matter whether your name is Smith or Zertuche, or whether your skin's black, brown, white, or purple. He loves you. He created you, and when you hate yourself, you're putting God down. God didn't make a mistake. The Bible says that God made you exactly the way He wanted you to be.[11] You need to ask Jesus to help you like yourself the way He made you, name and all."

We all gathered around Joe and prayed that he would let God heal the old hurts and help him learn to accept himself. The following morning, however, he walked away.

"I'm not ready yet," he said regretfully. "Maybe when I'm older, I'll come back."

"Joe was doing so good," Ninfa fought back the tears. "Why did he leave?"

"Joe needed the baptism in the Holy Spirit," I answered. "Jesus said, 'But you will receive power when the Holy Spirit comes on you....'[12] I believe every ex-drug addict needs to be baptized in the Holy Spirit. Without the power of the Holy Spirit, these guys can't make it; they need power to live the Christian life, power to resist temptation, power to witness, to teach, and to preach.

"We've got to teach and encourage them to seek the baptism in the Holy Spirit, to pray daily in English, in Spanish, and in tongues.[13]"

---

[11] Psalm 139:13-16 (NASB)

[12] Acts 1:8 (NIV)

[13] Acts 2:4 (NASB)

*　　　　　*　　　　　*

Juan Garza kicked his habit within a week, but he was still very irritable. He flared up easily and looked very discouraged. "I appreciate all you have done, Freddie," he told me, "but I don't feel at ease. I better leave."

"Let me ask you one thing," I stopped him. "Have you asked Jesus to forgive you for all of your sins?"

"I think so," Juan hesitated, "but I don't believe He hears me."

"Kneel down and repeat after me," I prompted him. "Jesus, I know that I am a lost sinner, and I ask forgiveness for all of my sins. I open the door to my heart and receive You as my Lord and Savior."

Juan repeated the words slowly and carefully. After a while, he got up with a smile, "Thank you for praying for me, Freddie."

The next morning he was singing loudly while doing his chores. "How do you feel, Juan?" I asked.

"¡De aquella!—Great!" he grinned. "Not only is the craving for heroin gone, Freddie, I don't even have the desire for a cigarette. I feel so clean inside, it seems like I never was a junkie."

"You know why?" I opened my Bible. "Here's how God's Word explains your change: 'Therefore if any man be in Christ, he is a new creature: old things are passed away; behold, all things are become new.'[14] That means that Jesus has made you a new person, Juan. He's given you new desires, a new mind, a new heart. You're not what you used to be."

---

[14] 2 Corinthians 5:17 (KJV)

"Thank You, Jesus!" He lifted up his hands, *"Gloria a Dios.*[h]*"*

In a few days Juan Garza received the baptism in the Holy Spirit.

\*　　　　\*　　　　\*

Every time the guys started singing to the Lord, my heart was touched. These were men who had used nothing but foul language and cursing; now they were singing about Jesus.

"I want you to form a choir," I told Ninfa.

"A choir?" she giggled. "The guys can't even carry a tune!"

"Just let them sing like they do here for chapel every morning," I was excited by the idea.

"But I don't know how to direct a choir," she protested.

"Then I'll do it!" I declared.

"You!" she exclaimed. "You don't know the first thing about music."

"Just watch me." I settled it once and for all. After a few "choir" practices, I took the guys out to Pastor Leo Villa's church.

Ninfa was waiting up for us when we returned. "How was it?" she looked concerned.

"Well, when they turned the service over to me, I called the choir up to the platform but forgot to tell them to use the side steps. They literally stampeded over the altar railing like a bunch of young colts jumping a fence," I roared with laughter.

"Oh, no!" Ninfa hid her face in her hands.

_____

[h] *Gloria a Dios.* – Glory to God.

"It was easy from then on," I assured her. "I turned to our guitar player and said, 'Give me a G.' I'd even instructed two guys to switch places when I said, 'First tenor and second tenor take your places, please.'"

"Where did you get that from?" Ninfa doubled up in laughter.

"When I was a kid, I heard some choir director say it, so I said it. But Ninfa," I grew serious, "when they started singing, the Lord anointed them. The presence of the Holy Spirit filled that place. The entire congregation was moved to tears."

"Thank You, Jesus," Ninfa whispered.

"It made me think of the first followers of Jesus," I continued. "They were '...uneducated and untrained men...,'[15] but He called them. He loved them. He discipled them. And I see Him doing it with our guys, Ninfa."

"Glory!" she exclaimed. "The Bible says, '...God has chosen the foolish things of the world to shame the wise....'[16] He couldn't have picked a better group than our wild bunch!"

---

[15] Acts 4:13 (NASB)
[16] 1 Corinthians 1:27 (NASB)

## Chapter 8

# Victory Home

Unless the Lord builds the house,
They labor in vain who build it.

Psalm 127:1 (NASB)

Addicts kept coming in, and the need for a larger home became urgent. Daily we prayed and searched for a place. When I found a two-bedroom home for rent, with option to buy, only a mile and a half away, I really got excited.

I took Ninfa to see it. Weeds grew tall all around the house. Inside, it was a mess, and globs of spittle had stained the walls and the floor. While we were there, a couple of scorpions and a few spiders scurried past our feet, making Ninfa squirm.

"The backyard must be the neighborhood dump," she murmured. "Look at all those junked cars."

"That's no problem," I assured her, "we can clean it up a little at a time. What I like about this property is that it's got two acres of land; our guys can get out and breathe."

We decided to rent, and prayed that if God wanted us to buy the house, He would provide money to buy it. With borrowed brooms, mops, and pails, we scraped, scrubbed, and cleaned. Outside, among the weeds in the backyard, we found the nest of a field mouse with eight, squeaking, baby mice.

"TINY!" Ninfa called our six-foot, three-hundred-pound guy and pointed to the nest. "Will you kill them?"

"No-o-o-o-o!" he replied firmly, "God made the poor little things; I can't kill them!" Before coming into the program, Tiny had stabbed a stoolie to death. Here was a murderer transformed by the power of Jesus Christ, unable to harm one of God's creatures.

"My God is real!" I rejoiced. *"Gloria a Dios.*[a] *"*

Before dark on the first day, I called the guys together. "Let's take time to praise Jesus," I told them. "Then, get some oil and anoint the house, over the doors, the windows, and on the walls; pray that the Holy Spirit will touch lives as they come here. Let's all lay hands on the house and dedicate it to the Lord."

"Amen!" the guys shouted, "Praise God!"

A week later, we were able to move in and open the doors of our new Victory Home at 1030 S.W. 39th Street. We flooded the streets of San Antonio with flyers making known our new address, and new addicts came in daily. Within a month thirty-five men were living with us.

A few women addicts were coming in also. They were sleeping with Ninfa and the children in the larger bedroom that doubled as our office and counselling room as well. The smaller bedroom was used for the men who came in to kick.[b]

I slept with the guys outside. We had cleaned up the ten junked cars in the backyard and used them as sleeping quarters. Some of us slept on cots or towels on the ground. All of us shared the one combined toilet and bathroom. On warm days, the guys showered

---

[a] *Gloria a Dios.* – Glory to God.
[b] kick – to withdraw from drugs

in the backyard with a water hose. To them, it was better than the streets, but I longed to give them adequate facilities. "Lord, I know the men can handle it," I prayed. "They're not complaining, but before winter comes, we're gonna have to build a dorm. Amen."

For the moment, I needed to take care of a minor but pressing matter; our guys needed haircuts.

Raider was back in town from Los Angeles, so I paid him a visit. As I walked into the barber shop, he greeted me, "I heard that you turned Alleluia."

"That's right," I answered. "I've been clean ever since Jesus Christ changed my life."

"I'm doing good too," Raider slurred, high on heroin.

"I need a barber," I told him. "I've got thirty-five men at the Victory Home. What kind of deal can you give me?"

"How about seventy-five cents a head?" he suggested. "I can go by once a week, all day. If you don't have the money that day, I'll let you slide on credit. Is that okay?"

"Thank You, Jesus," I replied.

"Thank you, Raider!" he joked.

Each time he came to the Home, every guy who got a haircut told him about Jesus. One day when he had finished work, Borrado and Güero offered to take him home. The three of them got into the car but never left. An hour later Raider walked back into Victory Home, red eyed and tear stained, but with a big smile, "I just asked Jesus into my heart; I'm staying so you can teach me about Him."

\*           \*           \*

Prisoners in county jail often asked me to be present in court during their trials. One morning I stepped out of the courtroom and bumped into a young, long-haired, *chicano*[c] hippie, high on drugs.

"Are you hooked?[d]" I asked outright.

Straightening up and forcing his eyes into focus, he slurred, "Sure am, man."

"My name is Freddie García. What's yours?"

With a haughty look, he boasted, "Juan Miguel Rivera."

"*Vamos a tomar guariche*–Let's go have some coffee," I suggested. On the way to the coffee stand, I asked him, "Have you ever heard of Victory Home?"

He lit a cigarette, took a deep drag, and slowly blew the smoke in my face. "Nope, never heard of it."

"It's a Home where drug addicts are staying clean," I explained.

He blew more smoke in my face, but before he could speak, I challenged him, "Do you wanna change?"

"Is an elephant fat?" he smirked. "Man, I've tried will power and the whole bit, but you know how it is."

"Look, Juan," I confronted him, "if you have the will to change, Jesus Christ can give you the power."

"Oh, man!" he grumbled. "My mom's always talking to me about that stuff."

"But have you tried it?" I insisted.

"Nope," he shrugged, "can't say I have."

"Here's my card with the address and phone number of Victory Home," I handed it to him. "Drop by and check it out. Jesus can really change your life."

Before the week was out, during morning chapel,

---

[c] *chicano* – a U.S. citizen of Mexican descent born in the United States

[d] hooked – addicted to drugs

Juan Miguel Rivera walked in. The only empty chair left was in the front row. Reluctantly, he sat down.

"Jesus said, 'Come to Me, all who are weary and heavy-laden, and I will give you rest,'[1]" I quoted from the Bible. "Jesus can break the bondage of drug addiction or of anything else that enslaves you. Is there anyone here this morning who feels in his heart the need to come to Jesus?"

Slowly, Juan lifted himself to his feet. He stood directly in front of me with his head bowed, but when I asked him to kneel, he glared at me with glassy eyes.

"Why do I have to kneel?" he slurred. "Why can't Jesus do whatever He's gonna do for me while I'm standing up?"

Firmly I placed my hand on his shoulder. "I wanna pray for you, Juan, that Jesus will come and make Himself real in your life."

He crumpled to the floor, "Jesus, forgive me for my sins and come into my life." Juan Rivera was finally home.

\*　　　　\*　　　　\*

"Lorenzo called," I announced to the guys. "He's coming to kick."

"Not Lorenzo the stoolie?" Lupe cautiously inquired. When I nodded, he jumped up from his chair. "The guy's a snitch, Freddie! He's a—"

"I know what he is, Lupe," I calmed him down. "But if he asks Jesus to forgive him, who are we to judge?"

When Lorenzo arrived, every single guy at the

---
[1] Matthew 11:28 (NASB)

Home gave him the silent treatment for days. No one would sit near him or talk to him. Finally during Bible study, I confronted them, "Do you know that Jesus tells us to love our enemies? And to do good to them that persecute us?"

"Man, Freddie, you're something else," Sammy protested. He pointed at Lorenzo, "These kind of guys are cold; they'd snitch on their own grandmothers! They don't care who gets hurt."

"But look at what the Bible says," I corrected him. "Jesus teaches us to pray to the Father, 'forgive us our sins, just as we have forgiven those who have sinned against us.'[2] As Christians we must learn to forgive those who hurt us, just as God has forgiven us."

Silence filled the room for what seemed a long time. Suddenly, Eddie's chair squeaked against the floor as he pushed it back and walked over to Lorenzo. "I was offered a contract to kill you," he confessed, "and even though I turned it down, I want you to forgive me for even thinking about it."

One by one the guys came to Lorenzo, asking his forgiveness, then turned to confess their offenses against each other.

"I stole your socks," Jaime told Lupe.

"And I stashed the soap for myself," Lupe admitted. "Please, forgive me."

"I want you to forgive me, Freddie," Sleepy stood before me, his face wet with tears. "I thought you were all phonies, so I came in just to prove you wrong. Please, forgive me."

"I forgive you," I embraced him.

Raider was standing nearby, and I felt the tugging

---

[2] Matthew 6:12 (TLB)

of the Holy Spirit in my heart. "Raider," I touched his shoulder, "the other day when I caught you parked in my driveway and scolded you, I did it with a bad attitude. Will you forgive me?"

"Yeah, man," he hugged me, "but I was wrong too. I knew the rules. Forgive me."

All around the room guys were hugging each other and crying. "Thank You, Jesus, for the convicting power of the Holy Spirit," I prayed. "Thank You for breaking our hardened hearts and for enabling us to forgive each other."

\*       \*       \*

Each morning after breakfast and chores, we came together for prayer from 10:00 to 10:30 a.m., followed by chapel service 'til noon. Immediately after lunch we held our daily Bible studies. One afternoon I was teaching on prayer, when one of the newer guys asked, "How do you pray, Freddie? I mean, what do you say?"

"Prayer is another word for communication," I explained. "God just wants you to speak to Him what you feel in your heart. Tell Him like it is; don't give Him no lip service. Tell Him about your doubts, your fears, your problems; God understands. And don't be surprised when He answers, 'cause He's gonna do it. It might be through a song, a testimony, a preaching or teaching, through His Word as you read it, or in a quiet voice in your heart, but I guarantee you, He'll talk right back to you."

"Give us an example," Ernie yelled, and the guys applauded.

"Well," I thought quickly, "we've got three turkeys in the freezer, but we need at least one more to make a meal for all of us. Let's pray right now that God will supply that turkey in Jesus' name 'cause I sure don't have the money to buy it."

"Amen!" the guys agreed. After we had prayed, I went on with the lesson. Our class was nearly over when a young man walked in.

"Hello there," he hollered. "Can you use a turkey, Freddie?"

I got goose bumps and began laughing when I saw that he was holding a turkey. "Thank You, Jesus!" I yelled. "Can we use a turkey, home boys?"

Several fellows stared at me, white faced and speechless. But the guys who had been with us for a while were used to seeing miracles; they whistled, clapped their hands, and praised Jesus. Soon the whole bunch joined in, thanking God. The young man had observed the scene in amazement, and I explained how the Lord had used him to answer prayer.

"I'm glad," he shook my hand. "I've been wanting to come by and see you for some time—do you remember me, Freddie?"

"No," I tried to place him. "Where did we meet?"

"I'm Polo. We went to elementary school together. When we were teenagers, you were in the Austin Street Gang. One night when you guys were high on something, one of the gang members pulled a gun on me, and you told him to shoot me. When he wouldn't do it, you said, 'Give me the gun; I'll shoot him!' I barely got away. Man, you guys were crazy!"

"Was that you, Polo?" I laughed. "Sure, I remember, and I'm sure glad Jesus changed me."

That evening I thanked the Lord all over again for the miracle He had done in my life:

"Where would I be today, Lord, if You hadn't

reached down Your hand for me? Where would we all be, Jesus, without Your mercy? We were once the rejects of society, men without initiative or purpose. But by the power of Your love, You've drawn us from under bridges, the prisons, the streets, from the gutter. From every walk of life, You've called us. We've come in filthy and wasted, with bent minds and broken bodies, and through Your blood shed on Calvary, You've set us free, filled us with new hope and the fire of the Holy Spirit. Thank You, Jesus," I prayed, "and help me, Lord, to lead them on the right path. Help me teach them to love and honor You, all the rest of their lives that they may learn to seek 'first the kingdom of God'[3] and Your righteousness, in Jesus' name, amen."

In Bible study the next day, I told the guys, "God is dependable and as His children, we've got to learn to be dependable too. That's why we require punctuality at prayer, chapel, and Bible studies. Jesus said, 'I am...the truth...,'[4] and as part of the family of God, we ought to speak and live truth. If you say you'll be someplace at 3:00 p.m., don't get there at 3:01. Learn to glorify Jesus in your punctuality and dependability.

"There was a time in our lives we were all irresponsible, undisciplined, and disorganized misfits of society but not no more. 'If any man be in Christ, he is a new creature: old things are passed away; behold, all things are become new.'[5]"

The guys roared in approval, "Thank You, Jesus!"

---

[3] Matthew 6:33 (KJV)

[4] John 14:6 (NASB)

[5] 2 Corinthians 5:17 (KJV)

They clapped and cheered me on.

When the room was quiet, I continued, "Jesus has made us clean inside, and that cleanliness should be seen on the outside. Remember when you were trying to look good for a chick?—how you shined your shoes and slicked your hair? Well, now you're working for the King of Kings and Lord of Lords, and you should look your best. You may not have a brand new suit, but whatever clothes you wear, make sure they're washed and ironed."

"Yes, amen!" they shouted.

"The same goes for this house," I went on. "It isn't fancy; everything in it is secondhand, but it all belongs to Jesus. That's why we scrub every room, sometimes twice a day, and there's always someone ready with a broom or a mop when the floor gets dirty or muddy. The Holy Spirit is changing lives and doing miracles every day in this little house; that's why we strive to keep it clean at all times!"

"There's power in the name of Jesus!" the class broke into praise and worship. "He's worthy to be praised."

Clean-up detail was not the most popular part of our routine, but it was an essential ingredient of discipline. When someone broke one of the rules, he was assigned to scrub the bathroom, do dishes, wash windows, or clean the yard for a week, longer if the offense was serious. Complaints automatically extended the discipline.

"Man, this is worse than boot camp," the guys joked around. *"Se salen.*e*"*

"That's funny," I replied. "Some of you have done

---

e *Se salen.* – They're out of line.

five, ten, fifteen years in prison, picking cotton in the hot sun, for the devil's sake. But when it comes to being disciplined while you're in training for Jesus, you start sniveling or you wanna quit.

"Sure this is like boot camp. It ain't a Boy Scout camp. We're in the army of the Lord; if there's no discipline, you don't have an army, you have a mob! Our schedule and rules may seem strict at first, but they are set up to help you develop the character of Christ in your life."

Prayer was at the heart of all our discipline. "It works two ways," I told the guys. "Prayer gives us the power to live a disciplined life. The outward discipline strengthens our prayer life."

Prayer was the first thing we impressed on our newcomers; the more time they spent in prayer, the easier it became to live according to God's Word. Nothing was done without prayer.

"When you're out there on the streets and in the schools and prisons witnessing about Jesus, you're in the combat zone. You're doing battle with Satan himself for the souls of men," I coached them. "The power to set men free belongs to Jesus, and He says, 'Without Me [you] can do nothing.'[6] We have no business out there without spending time in prayer first."

Throughout the day and often late at night, small groups of guys would gather to pray; we would hear their voices rising and falling, praying in English, in Spanish, and in tongues. While some of us were out witnessing, others would be at home praying; there was strength in knowing they were fighting a spiritual battle for us.

---

[6] John 15:5 (KJV)

Often Ninfa stayed home alone with our children, preparing supper, while I took the guys to evening services at local churches. One evening she told me, "When the kitchen door leading to the backyard is left open after dark, I sometimes sense an icy-cold fear looming out there."

I laughed at her remark, but when I shared it with the guys, they confessed to sensing an eerie presence too. We had dedicated the Home to the Lord, but we hadn't claimed the two acres of land. I knew that the property had once been used as a drug connection. Evil had ruled.

"We're gonna claim every inch of this land for Jesus!" I challenged the guys. "The Bible says that God has 'not given us the spirit of fear; but of power,...and of a sound mind.'[7] So let's walk out into that darkness in Jesus' name and pray, 'til His presence fills the land."

The guys cheered and whistled and teamed up as prayer partners, heading outside. They fell to their knees and began praising Jesus in English, in Spanish, and in tongues. Night after night they ventured farther out. Soon we could open our windows late at night and hear their voices resounding with chants of prayer and praise to Jesus Christ throughout the entire two acres.

"The fear is gone!" Ninfa remarked in wonder one evening. "You can sense God's presence surrounding us. The whole area is like a sanctuary."

"Praise Him!" I called out the window into the night, and from outside, some of the guys responded, "Praise Jesus! Alleluia! There's power in the name of

---

[7] 2 Timothy 1:7 (KJV)

Jesus!"

A few days later, Manuel Zertuche, Juan Rivera, Juan Garza, and José Luis Flores approached me. "Several of the men want to take turns fasting and praying so that there will be a continual chain of prayer going on around the clock, day and night," they told me. "We've got a list of volunteers already. During the night, the guys who pray one 'watch' will wake up the next fellows on the list; then they'll do the same for the next group. There'll never be a time when someone ain't praying in this place."

"Thank You, Jesus!" I raised my hands. "Let's do it."

Our enthusiasm grew from day to day. On the roof of the house, facing the street, the guys had put up a sign: "Expect a Miracle." You could walk all over the two acres and feel the presence of the Lord. Even strangers felt it, as soon as they stepped inside the gate.

One day we were holding chapel services in the living room. Some ex-addicts were crowded into the narrow pews and chairs, and some were standing along the walls, by the open windows and in doorways. Ninfa was playing the piano, and we were all singing when Raider spotted the mailman coming through the gate. The minute he stepped inside the fence, he fell to his knees. Manuel Zertuche, Juan Rivera, and Raider ran to him ahead of the others. "Do you want to repent of your sins and accept Jesus as your Savior?" Raider asked him.

"Yes! Yes!" he sobbed.

While they were praying with him, an old-time evangelist drove up. As soon as he set foot in the front yard and saw what was happening, he started jumping and shouting: "This is holy ground! This is holy ground!"

Within minutes all the guys had come streaming out of chapel and joined in jumping and hollering. "This is holy ground! There is power in the name of Jesus!"

The mailman took a pack of cigarettes from his shirt pocket and handed it to Raider. Juan Rivera shouted, "Give me one of those cigarettes," and the guys echoed him, "Yeah, give me one too!"

"The spoils of war" were handed out, and soon the guys were tearing up cigarettes. Still jumping, they continued, "Alleluia! There's power in the blood of Jesus!" The mailman joined in, and after much rejoicing, he finally went on his way down the street with a big grin on his face and the love of God in his heart.

Another day, while we were in chapel, Juan Rivera's grandmother walked in while the worship service was going on. Immediately she fell to her knees. We prayed with her and she gave her life to Christ. Afterwards she told us what had happened. "When I came into the room where you were praying and praising God, I saw angels standing over in the corners, and I knew that God was here."

Such miracles happened daily, and the faith and confidence of our guys grew with each occurrence. They headed for the streets to witness for Christ, and when the van came back, it sounded like the return of a football team after winning a game. They told of addicts falling to their knees on the sidewalk to ask Jesus into their lives. Often the new convert came home with them to kick his drug habit.

We were still living on a shoestring; our shelves in the kitchen were as empty now as when we first started in our small house on San Eduardo Street. But the guys were sure that God would meet every need.

On the wall in the office, we posted our prayer requests. We needed to pay the rent and the water, gas, and electric bills. We also needed groceries and supplies, clothing, and repairs. Sometimes people came with money; other times they brought the specific items we had prayed for or offered their services.

One morning Ninfa told me we were low on sugar. I put it on our list, and a few days later a woman walked into the living room. "Could you use a hundred pounds of sugar?" Before Ninfa had time to answer, the woman continued: "I work for a restaurant, and the other day a supplier brought a bag of sugar that was torn a little. The restaurant owner didn't want to purchase it, and the trucker said I could have it for a couple of dollars. I'd heard of your ministry and bought it for you."

Ninfa smiled and told the woman, "We've been praying for sugar. The Lord used you to supply it."

It was the visitor's turn to rejoice. "Praise God!" she exclaimed. "I'm so grateful that He was able to use my life to meet your needs."

Immediately after chapel service one morning, a young man came to the office. "Freddie, my name is Rogelio," he smiled and shook my hand. "My brother Tomás is in your program. Is it okay if I give him a pair of shoes I bought for him?"

"*Seguro*–Sure," I smiled, "let me call him in."

A few minutes later Tomás walked into the office, with Juan Rivera close behind him. When Tomás received the shoe box, Juan's eyes widened.

"Thank You, Jesus!" Tomás held up his brand new shoes for all to see, "That's exactly what I prayed for!"

Juan Rivera later revealed, "I was kneeling beside Tomás when he prayed for those shoes. But what blew me away is that he asked the Lord for a pair of tangerine Stacy Adams." Juan shook his head. "I was sure Tomás was in for a disappointment, but when I saw the Stacy Adams shoe box, I knew they were going to be tangerine!" When the rest of the guys heard what had happened, they almost raised the roof with their cheers of praise.

We were excited to see how the Lord provided what we asked for, but I reminded the guys again and again that our prayers were meant first of all to bring us into the presence of God. "'Seek ye first the kingdom of God, and His righteousness,'[8]" I told them. "Righteousness means 'living right,' living a life of holiness and commitment before God. When we do that, He will give us what we need."

They started to cheer, but I quieted them, "Listen to what I said. He gives you what you need, not always what you want. You might selfishly be asking Him for a Cadillac, when you need to ask Him to help you love your brother. Serve and honor God because He is God, not because you are interested in the material things He can give you."

They understood but were still as exuberant as little children each time they saw answered prayer.

We prayed for the practical needs of the ministry, but we prayed first and last for souls still in bondage. Sometimes during prayer, the presence of the Holy Spirit was so strong that any demon-possessed person there was set free.

---

[8] Matthew 6:33 (KJV)

Homosexuality was rare among those who came to our program, but those who stayed were set free from their sexual deviation when they accepted Christ. Chris was a homosexual who sought help in the Home. When he came in I told him, "Homosexuality is not your problem; sin is your problem. When you ask Jesus to forgive you for your sins, He will deliver you from the bondage of abnormal sexuality."

We started fasting and praying that God would manifest His power to this young man. One morning during chapel when we were all praying and praising Jesus, we heard a chilling scream and felt the presence of something evil. There on the floor lay Chris spitting and cursing at us, his eyes glinting red through narrow lids. Several of the newer guys jumped back and I told them: "Any of you who are not prayed up, or who are afraid, don't stay. Leave the room. The rest of you gather around Chris and let's pray!"

A few left, while the rest of us started praying in Spanish, in English, and in tongues. Chris lashed at some of us with claw-like fingers and tried to bite one of the Bibles. We laid hands on him, and I told him, "Listen to me, Chris. I'm gonna pray for you, and while I'm praying, you ask Jesus to forgive you for all of your sins." Then I went on to address the demon within him: "You foul, unclean spirit, I command you in the name of Jesus Christ of Nazareth to come out of him."

Chris went limp and we lifted him up. His eyes were clear and he straightened his shoulders. I held up his hands. "Praise Jesus for setting you free, Chris. Praise Him," I instructed him. He began to walk around the room with hands uplifted, praising

God. The evidence of his deliverance was visible to all of us; his effeminate walk was gone. The guys danced and shouted. "*¡Gloria a Dios!* Thank You, Jesus! There is power in the blood of Jesus! *A su Nombre gloria.*[f]"

\*       \*       \*

"I've rented the Lanier High School Auditorium, Ninfa," I rushed into our bedroom excitedly. "We're gonna have a city-wide crusade, and our choir is gonna sing!"

"But, Freddie," Ninfa looked worried, "our guys can't really sing that well, remember?"

"San Antonio has never seen such a thing as a 'cured' drug addict," I pointed out, "much less an 'Ex-Addict Choir.' The people in our *barrio*[g] need to know that Jesus is still in the miracle-making business." Ninfa said nothing, and I urged her, "You direct the choir; I'll take care of literature and promotion."

She looked as if she wanted to protest but instead threw up her hands and giggled, "Here we go again!"

"Look, Ninfa," I assured her, "you know music and they are comfortable with you. They'll sing their best and God will be glorified."

I was full of enthusiasm. Radio and TV announced the up-coming event; our guys were praying continually, and the choir under Ninfa's direction sounded great. Finally the big day arrived. We were all a little nervous backstage; we'd never held a crusade before. When the doors to the auditorium were opened, Ninfa and I peeked through the curtains. "Look at all the

---

[f] *A su Nombre gloria.* – Glory to His name.

[g] *barrio* – neighborhood

people, Freddie. They must be coming in bus loads!"

The seating capacity in the auditorium was 1,200, but to our amazement it was packed; people were standing along the walls, and teenagers were sitting on the floor in the aisles. Before the curtain went up, we held hands and prayed. Then Father Renfro, the Catholic priest, gave the *bienvenida*[h] and the invocation. He then introduced us, and Ninfa walked to the piano while our choir, dressed in white shirts and dark pants, lined up on stage.

From the first song to the last, their voices lifted up the name of Jesus. They concluded by singing, "Without Him I would be nothing; without Him I'd surely fail..." They sang it through once, then hummed the melody while two of them came to the microphone and told the story of their release from drugs. They wept as they spoke, and there was hardly a dry eye in the audience. Never, in the history of San Antonio, had anything like this been seen before.

My sermon was entitled, "The Wages of Sin." When I concluded, about three hundred young people accepted Jesus as their Savior.

On our way home, I said, "Ninfa, do you realize that the only 'public appearance' our guys ever made before was in court when they faced a judge and jury?" She and I both laughed and thanked Jesus for what had taken place that night.

We were exhausted, and once we got home, I headed straight for bed. When I took off my shoes, Ninfa exclaimed, "You mean to tell me that you went up on stage wearing a new suit and tie without no socks?"

I laughed. "I ain't got no underwear either! I didn't

---

[h] *bienvenida* – the welcoming address

find any clean ones in my drawer, and I really didn't have time to go buy a new pair."

"Are you implying that it's my fault?" she was defensive.

"No," I sighed, "I ain't trying to imply anything. I'm very tired, Ninfa; let's just go to sleep."

In a sudden burst of anger, Ninfa yelled, "Why didn't you let me know you needed clean socks, instead of making me feel guilty?!"

"I don't have to let you know anything!" I snapped back. "You're old enough to know that your responsibility is to have my clothes ready!"

Ninfa was furious. "Have you ever stopped to consider why they're not ready?" she screamed. "Look at the many jobs you've got me doing. Yet, instead of showing a little consideration, you get on my case!"

That was the last straw. I sat up in bed and lashed out: "You want to argue about consideration? When have you heard me complain about the many times I've worn the same shirt for days? And when it comes to breakfast, lunch, or supper, it seems like I married the *taco*[i] place down the street, not a wife. You're never around, Ninfa, not for me nor the kids. You're always too busy coming or going, helping someone else."

Neither of us said another word. We went to bed and turned our backs toward each other. *What are we doing wrong?* I pleaded in prayer. *Why are we drifting apart?*

Next morning during chapel, Ninfa and I asked each other's forgiveness. Later we took time to talk. "What's happening to us, Freddie?" Ninfa's eyes filled

---

[i] *taco* – flour tortilla with various fillings

with tears. "When we first became Christians, things were great. Lately, all we do when we get together is disagree, and now we're starting to fight."

"I know," I pulled her close to me and wiped her tears. "And I don't have an answer; we both need to seek the Lord, and ask Him to show us what we're doing wrong. I love you very much, Ninfa, and I care about what happens to our marriage. I don't want to waste precious years bickering with you. God is using our lives, and this should be a time of rejoicing for you and me."

We held each other close, determined to pray and seek God's Word for an answer to our problem.

# Chapter 9

# Victory Temple

Upon this rock I will build My church;
and the gates of Hades shall not overpower it.

Matthew 16:18b (NASB)

"A what!?!" Ninfa burst out and almost choked on
her *enchilada*.[a]

"Shhhh! We're at a restaurant," I reminded her.
Calmly, I repeated myself, "I feel in my heart that
God wants me to pastor a church, and I'm gonna do
it."

"Oh, no, I can't be a pastor's wife!" she exploded. "I
love cooking and washing for all the fellows, but that's
as far as it goes. Me, a pastor's wife? Forget it, Freddie. I don't talk, look, or feel like one. This one time,
you can count me out."

"How do you think I feel, Ninfa? I don't know how to
pastor, but I'm all they've got," I reasoned. "We can't
ignore the need. Guys who accept Christ and complete the program go home and start bumming from
church to church. I've told them again and again how
important it is to become a member of a church, but
they don't do it. In our program they learn how to get
rooted in the Word of God, but it's just as important to
become responsible church members. If there's no
commitment, there's no responsibility–not to God,
not to anyone. They will begin to slack off and may

---

[a] *enchilada* – corn tortilla with cheese and onion filling, covered
with red chili sauce

even end up back on the streets again."

"I know what you're saying is true," Ninfa admitted, "but—"

I didn't let her finish, "Think how hard it must be for a new Christian to go home to an unbelieving mate. The Christian wants to go to a prayer meeting while the unbelieving mate considers it a bore and wants to go someplace else. This problem won't end 'til the entire family comes to know Jesus as their Savior.

"How can they all be reached?" I concluded. "Through the church! We need a community church that will reach out, not just to the drug addicts but to their entire families; I mean kids and all, plus their friends and neighbors."

"I still can't picture myself as a pastor's wife," Ninfa sighed then smiled, "but in Jesus' name, here we go again!"

Right away we began looking on Guadalupe Street for a place to hold our church meetings. Day in and day out, we searched up and down the same street hoping to see a vacant building. "Why not look somewhere else?" Ninfa was worn out. "There's nothing here but *cantinas*.[b]"

"This is where the need is," I explained. "This is Satan's backyard. Besides, it's all we can afford."

"Amen to that," she chuckled.

Finally one day we saw someone moving out of a storefront building. We stopped and introduced ourselves. "We saw you cleaning out," I began. "Is this building for rent?"

The man didn't answer but turned and walked

---

[b] *cantinas* – beer joints

inside. We followed. The large room was dark and stuffy with two single windows by the back door.

"I'm a minister, sir," I said, hoping to impress him. "I work with drug addicts and their families."

"What'cha want the place for? To work with addicts?" He looked worried.

"No, no," I assured him. "Your building would be used as a church."

Ninfa had been looking around the room. "Was this a church once?" she asked the man.

"No, ma'am," he grinned, "this was known as 'Las Aguilas Bar.' Why do you ask?"

"I thought that was the altar section," she pointed to a small platform in the back.

"No, ma'am," he chuckled, "that was the bandstand."

We all laughed and it helped break the ice. The man's name was Julio, and he patiently heard us out as we told him about Jesus. He agreed to think about letting us rent the building. The minute we got home we told the guys, and they joined us in praying that God would place in Julio's heart to say yes.

He called a few days later, "Mr. García, give me a week to fix the rest rooms and you can move in."

"Thank You, Jesus!" I shouted as I hung up the phone. "Get the guys together," I told Juan Rivera. "We got the building!"

"Yea!!" they roared in excitement, "*¡Gracias, Señor!*–Thank You, Lord!"

"It's gonna need some fixing," I explained when they quieted down, "and this is what we're gonna do. God has given each of you different talents. Some of you are carpenters, electricians, or painters. This is your church, and it needs your talent now, and for as long as you're a member."

They worked vigorously for almost a month, cleaning, painting, and repairing. Two guys built a wall to partition off an entry. Sammy was a carpet layer. He went to several carpet companies and asked for remnants, then covered the altar section with a beautiful patchwork of different colors and sizes. Manuel Zertuche built a pulpit in the shape of a cross.

Behind the building was a small house we had rented for twenty-five dollars a month. There the children's church would meet. Some of the guys volunteered to build child-size pews and decorate the small rooms with donated paint in different colors. While we all worked to get the church ready, Lee, an ex-alcoholic, was voted the cook for the work crew.

Late one evening, I drove down Guadalupe Street to check on the guys who were still working at the church. *Conjunto* music blared from juke boxes and dance bands. Large neon signs advertised the beer joints and dance halls. I couldn't help but notice the contrast with our plain storefront church, with one single light bulb over the door. I felt anger rising inside. "God deserves the spotlight," I told myself aloud. "Let the devil take the back seat!"

When I got to the church, I shared my idea with the guys: "We're gonna rig up loudspeakers outside, so everybody on the streets can hear our preaching and music, and I'll order a big neon sign for the front that'll say VICTORY TEMPLE."

The guys cheered, and I continued, "We're gonna put a juke box just inside the door so people can see it from the street. It'll play English and Spanish songs. The only difference is that this 'converted' juke box is gonna play nothing but gospel music!

"On the other side of the entrance, also visible from

the street, we'll put a small bar with bar stools–a 'converted' bar. We'll use it when we don't have church service, to serve free Kool-Aid and coffee, cookies, and donuts to anyone who walks in. And we can tell them about Jesus!"

On Mother's Day, we held our first service. The building was packed with ex-addicts and their families. "This church is a perfect gift for Mother's Day," I spoke from the pulpit. "Nearly every day I get a call from a mother–'Can you help my daughter, she's in the streets; can you help my son, he's an addict.' Now God has answered their prayers and opened a church where their sons and daughters can be reached with the gospel of Jesus Christ!"

On a Sunday morning, before the worship service started, Mama walked into Victory Temple. My niece, Lizzy, a Christian, had invited her to come. Directly behind them entered sixteen Anglo Christians who'd come from out of town to worship the Lord with us. Mama had visited the church before but still had not accepted Jesus as her Savior.

"Oh, Lord," I prayed, "I've got a problem. If I preach in Spanish for my mother's sake, our English-speaking friends will not be ministered to. Yet if I speak in English for their sake, Lord, Mama will not understand the message of salvation. Please, tell me what to do."

The worship service started, and as I got ready to speak, I felt the prompting of the Holy Spirit to preach in English. I obeyed, and after the sermon, much to my surprise, Mama was among those who came forward and knelt at the altar.

I saw the tears in her eyes and hurried to her. Placing my hand on her head, I whispered in her ear, "Ask

Jesus to forgive you for your sins, Mama." She prayed softly and remained at the altar, weeping silently.

Afterwards, I led her up on the platform. "How do you feel, Mama?"

Her face was still wet with tears. "Fine," she replied shyly.

I hugged her. "Did you accept Jesus as your Savior?"

Looking up, she smiled and nodded, *"Sí.*[c]*"*

\*　　　\*　　　\*

Mama's faithful presence in the church made me more aware of the need to make our services bilingual. The younger generation of Mexican-Americans who spoke little Spanish wanted to have their worship services in English; however, many of our older people wanted the preaching and teaching in Spanish. To meet this need we started having two services on Sunday, one in Spanish and the other in English; we also sang the same hymns and choruses in both languages. During the week, we followed the same pattern for our meetings and Bible studies.

The bilingual arrangement served two purposes: everyone was comfortable being taught God's Word in their own language, yet they were exposed to the other; those who spoke only Spanish were learning English and vice versa.

\*　　　\*　　　\*

"Freddie," Manuel Zertuche approached me one morning, "I want to talk with you."

---

[c] *Sí* – yes

"What's up?"

"Last night, the guys got to talking in the dorm, and Raider told us that he'd like to go to Bible school. It made me realize that I want to go too."

"Praise the Lord!" I was all for it.

"That's not all," he added with a smile. "Juan Rivera and Juan Garza want to go also."

"Call them over here," I urged him. "I wanna have a talk with all of you."

They gathered around, anxious for a word of counsel. "Only the Holy Spirit can put the hunger in your hearts to learn more of God's Word," I encouraged them. "So, fill in your application to the school of your choice and get ready to go." None of the guys had the money, but by faith, seven of them registered; before long, their tuition had been provided.

All seven were in the choir, and I was afraid we would never get them all together again. Now was the time to record an album. After prayer the following morning, I broke the news, "You guys are the first fruits of this ministry. Soon, there will be a new crop of fellows coming into the Home. I believe the Victory Ex-Addict Choir should leave behind a witness in song about Jesus, so others may be inspired to go on."

"Sounds great!" Manuel Zertuche agreed, "but do you think we can make it? We leave for Bible school in two months."

"We'll practice every day and be ready in one month," I smiled. "Just get together with Ninfa and see what songs you'd like to sing."

She drilled them several hours daily, and in August we all trooped into the recording studio. The guys were getting nervous in the sound room while technicians arranged the microphones. "Remember why you're here," I told them. "We're not here because we sing so beautifully; there are other people who can sing better than us. The only thing that pleases the Lord about us is that we sing to Him from the bottom of our hearts. So remember where He picked us up from, and praise Him with a grateful heart."

One of the solos Ninfa sang was "It Took A Miracle," and we chose it as the title song for our album. It took a miracle for God to change our lives; our album was a miracle in itself.

On their last day at Victory Home, during morning chapel, we laid hands on our seven students and prayed. After the service, Juan Garza pulled Ninfa aside. I could tell by the look on her face that he was making her upset, so I joined them. She pointed to Juan, "He doesn't want to go to Bible school."

"It's not that I don't want to go, Freddie," he shook his head. "It's just that, well...I don't know how to tell you. It's just that I'm too dumb."

"Who said you were dumb?" I was surprised.

He looked embarrassed and hung his head. "I've always been dumb, Freddie. I dropped out of school because I was never able to make good grades." Juan began describing his childhood, each word echoing my own story. "I love the Lord, Freddie," he choked back tears, "and that's why I don't want to cheat Him. Someone else who is smarter than me should go in my place. Jesus really deserves the best."

Patting him on the shoulder, I said, "*Vente*–Come with me–to the backyard." We settled ourselves under a shade tree. "Listen, Juan, any man who is able to steal over two hundred dollars a day to support his heroin habit–without getting caught–has to have a brain. So don't tell me you're dumb," I chuckled.

"Now, if you tell me you don't like to study, then that's a different story. I'll be the first one to tell you not to go to Bible school 'cause you'll be wasting your time and the Lord's, but don't shortchange yourself thinking you're dumb, 'cause that's not true."

Juan listened attentively and I went on. "Don't you realize that the all-powerful Creator of the universe lives in your heart? And, don't you remember that the Bible teaches us, 'I can do all things through Christ which strengtheneth me.'[1]"

"Yes, sir," he replied meekly.

"Well, then," I concluded, "don't tell me you can't do it. Apply God's Word to your life, go on to Bible school, and shine for Jesus."

"Yes, sir!" There was a new determination in his eyes. "*Muchas gracias*–Thank you very much, Freddie."

When our Bible-school students left, there were thirty-five new guys at Victory Home. Cold weather was coming, and my biggest concern was the fifteen guys sleeping outside in the junked cars. We had eight bunks in a tiny house trailer parked in the back, and there were men sleeping on the couches and on the floor in the living room.

We needed to add a dorm badly, but we couldn't build on rented property, and we had no money to purchase it. "Jesus," I prayed, "You've met all our needs. I thank You and ask You to help us now."

One day an elderly Christian woman came to see me. Her face radiated kindness. She handed me a check, "God impressed on my heart to give you the money to be used as a down payment to buy this property for the Lord's work," she smiled. "The one thing I

---

[1] Philippians 4:13 (KJV)

ask, Freddie, is that you never mention my name. This is between the Lord and me."

I knew she wasn't a wealthy woman; she wasn't even a member of our church. But when I found out that she had sold her own house and was moving in with her sister in order to provide us with the money, I was deeply touched. Her gift was a sacrifice of love. "Thank You, Jesus," I prayed when she left. "Thank You that there are people who care."

The five thousand dollars paid nearly half of the sum of purchase. But when I told Ninfa I wanted to build a dorm, she threw up her hands in despair. "In that case, you get someone else to take care of your bookkeeping," she sighed. "I don't know how to balance in the 'red.'"

I was determined. "Winter is coming and I don't have a place to put the guys. I have to build now. I'm going to order the cement and get ready to pour the slab. God knows that this is not a foolish expense. I believe the money will come in. If not, we'll just go back to San Eduardo Street."

When the guys heard of my plans, they offered to help: "I can dig the foundation, I can work with concrete, I'm a brick layer, I'm a plumber, I'm an electrician, I'm a carpenter."

"Look," I told Ninfa, "the Lord has put the workmen right here among us. He'll supply the funds for materials as we go along."

Within a week, we poured the slab. It was all we could afford, but we were elated to have at least started. We had faith that, little by little, the block walls would go up, then the roof. We believed it all would be finished by Christmas.

\*　　　　\*　　　　\*

Our new guys had a gung ho attitude. They were eager to be in chapel and in Bible study. They carried their Bibles with them and were always ready to share Scriptures and preach to each other. When a stranger walked into Victory Home, they flocked around, wanting to be the first to tell him about Jesus.

I knew that several of them felt the call to go into the work of the Lord full-time, but I was surprised when Ramón approached me. "Freddie, I want to do something for Jesus now. Send me to open up a Victory Home in El Paso, Texas." Before I could say a word, he added, "There are lots of junkies in that city who've never heard the gospel."

Ramón's plan seemed to be in line with the vision God had placed in my own heart. By faith I'd seen Victory Homes all over Texas; perhaps this was the beginning.

"I won't be able to help you out too much financially," I cautioned him.

"You've taught us to trust in God," he replied. "All I want is your counsel and guidance along the way."

A few days later we laid hands on Ramón and wished him Godspeed as he left for El Paso.

I put my arm around Ninfa, "We have actually launched out our first spiritual son into full-time ministry, and it sure feels good."

"I'm excited about it too," she smiled up at me, "but it's sad to see him leave."

"You can't stop him," I reminded her. "You can't stop any of them. Our job is to help them find God's will for their lives, then let them go. Don't worry about Ramón. I'll coach him along the way and teach him what the Lord has taught me. In Jesus' name he'll do well."

In less than a month, Ramón was the talk of the town in El Paso. He was interviewed by newspapers, radio, and TV and was given a house, rent-free. It was soon filled with drug addicts. His instant success, however, turned into our heartache.

"Ramón," I called him long distance, "there's a guy on his way to El Paso, and I want you to be careful. He doesn't want anything to do with the things of God. He's a rebel, an instigator, and a freeloader. My advice to you is not to receive him; he can tear down your whole ministry."

"You take care of San Antonio; that's your turf, Freddie," Ramón was defiant. "Here in El Paso, I'm in charge. I'll take whoever I want. I'm not interested in being under authority anymore—I'm going on my own."

"Man!" I scolded myself when I hung up the phone, "now I understand why the Apostle Paul warned not to place a novice in leadership.[2]" Fearfully I went down on my knees and prayed, "Lord, I'm at fault for having permitted Ramón to start a work before he was ready."

Soon afterwards, we began hearing that Ramón's ministry was in trouble. I determined not to make the same mistake again.

\*         \*         \*

When the stores downtown began to decorate for Christmas, I got the guys together after chapel. "I'm gonna teach you how to do street rallies," I

---

[2] 1 Timothy 3:6 (KJV)

announced. "We don't have the money to print up flyers to advertise, but downtown is crowded with Christmas shoppers already; we'll do our rallies there."

The guys applauded and shouted, "Let's go for it!"

"Jesus says, '...Follow Me, and I will make you fishers of men,'[3]" I pointed to my open Bible. "Our job is to go where the 'fish' are: in the streets, ghettos, *barrios*[d]—wherever sin is. People are hurting and it's our job to take them the healing gospel of Jesus Christ."

It took us a couple of days to get everything together. Ninfa rehearsed Christmas carols with the guys, and I borrowed a Santa Claus outfit. Henry, a large, heavy-set ex-addict was willing to play Santa.

"Our plan of action is simple," I told them when we were ready. "You guys that want to be preachers watch how I do it. We'll set up with microphones and speakers on a busy corner downtown and start singing Christmas carols. Meanwhile, Santa will be on the sidewalk passing out candy, and the little kids will bring their parents to see him. When we get a crowd together, I'll call a couple of you fellows to testify. Then I'll preach and make an invitation to accept Jesus."

Our Christmas street rallies were a great hit. When the crowd of shoppers thinned out in the evenings, we headed for the *barrios* and sang Christmas carols on Guadalupe Street and at the homes of the drug pushers.[e] Some came out to greet us, offered us coffee, and listened with tears as we sang and told

---

[3] Matthew 4:19 (NASB)

[d] *barrio* – neighborhood

[e] pusher – person who sells drugs

them about Jesus.

About a week before Christmas, as Josie and Paul were getting ready for bed, I took Paul on my lap while Josie curled up next to Ninfa. "Tell me," I asked them, "what have you two decided you want for Christmas?"

Without hesitation Paul replied, "I want a room all to myself so I can go to sleep when I want to."

To hear my six-year-old son ask for privacy, rather than a toy, hurt. There was no way I could give him what he wanted. With a lump in my throat, I turned to Josie. "What about you, *mi hija*?[f]"

She smiled shyly and shrugged her shoulders, "I don't know what I want, Papa."

"Well, then," I hugged them both, "we'll just have to wait 'til Christmas to find out what Jesus will bring you."

Christmas vacation brought our Bible-school students home for the holidays. We had a surprise for them; the new dorm and dining room stood ready. We would eat our traditional Christmas dinner there. "Man!" Juan Rivera yelled when he walked in and saw the new structure, "you guys have it made! We had to sleep outside!"

"Praise the Lord!" one of our newer guys smiled, "but the blessings of the Lord didn't come 'til you guys left." We all roared with laughter and welcomed our students home.

On Christmas Eve day, Ninfa started to cook the meat for the *tamales*[g] at three o'clock in the morning.

---

[f] *mi hija* – my daughter

[g] *tamales* – seasoned corn dough, filled with spiced, chopped meat, wrapped in softened corn husks and steamed

Mama arrived at dawn, and while Ninfa chopped and spiced the meat, Mama prepared the corn *masa*.[h]

Soon after daylight the mothers and wives of our men, with all the children, came to set up our "assembly line" in the dining room. Some spread the *masa* on the softened corn shucks; others added the meat and folded the *tamales*; a third group packed five-gallon drums with twenty dozen *tamales* in each and poured boiling hot meat broth over them. The guys then carried the covered drums outside. They placed them in open fire pits, where Petra, one of our church women, was in charge of the final stage of cooking. The other guys were responsible for preparing two fifty-gallon drums of *menudo*.[i] Back in the kitchen, big pots of Mexican rice and beans were simmering on the stove.

Towards evening, when everything was ready for the meal, our Victory family—about 350 of us counting the children—held our Christmas Eve worship service. The adults were packed together in the living room and office, with some of the men standing in the doorways. The children had their service outside under the carport; their colorful *piñatas*[j] that hung from the roof were homemade.

The entire house was decorated with garlands of red tinsel and a few donated Christmas ornaments. In a corner of the living room stood the donated tree the fellows had cut down themselves and helped decorate. For many of our guys it was their first celebration of Christmas outside the penitentiary; others

---

[h] *masa* – seasoned corn dough

[i] *menudo* – Mexican spiced soup made of calf's abdominal lining with pig's feet, hominy, and red chili pods

[j] *piñatas* – a decorated, hollow container in varied shapes, made of thin, plaster-like mixture, filled with candy; used in parties

had lived on the streets for years. For all our newcomers, it was their first Christmas with Jesus Christ.

After our worship, we held our traditional feast in the new dining room. Many had to stand up while they ate. It was obvious already that our building program had only begun.

Early Christmas morning, Josie and Paul were up to open their gifts. Mama had given us the money to buy them. Paul's eyes shone when he saw his "new" second-hand bike, and Josie immediately put on her little girl's necklace and earrings and set out her toy dishes. Both had planned a surprise for me. Paul proudly handed me the big package, wrapped in aluminum foil from the kitchen. "Here, Dad, this is from me and Josie," he beamed.

They watched eagerly, as I unwrapped my gift and found a green, traveler's garment bag. "It's for when you get to go preach out of town," Josie excitedly explained. "We picked it out ourselves."

I hugged them both and assured them that theirs was the best gift of all. Later, Ninfa told me how the children had prayed that Jesus would help them get the perfect gift for Daddy and had carefully searched through several large boxes of donated clothing to find it.

Before the day was over, Frankie, Ricky, and Sandra had arrived to spend the rest of the holidays with us. The only one of our children missing was Jesse. We prayed that one day we would all be together.

\*       \*       \*

Our seven students returned to Bible school just after New Year's. "Now that they're gone," I told Ninfa, "I'm gonna concentrate more on discipling new guys."

I had already started to disciple[k] Gilbert. He had become addicted to heroin while serving as a sergeant in Vietnam. The day he walked into Victory Home he was so sick that when he knelt to accept Jesus into his life, he had to lean against another fellow just to keep from falling over. Christ healed him of his addiction instantly.

Now he had asked if I would take him under my wing and train him to become a preacher without sending him to Bible school. It was a challenge I intended to accept. "From now on, I'm gonna involve Gilbert with me in the church and the Home," I told Ninfa. "I'll take him along when I speak in jails, schools, civic clubs, and other churches. Whatever I do, he will do."

Ninfa had listened and nodded in agreement. Now I added: "There's something else we need to do; start teaching in the church on Christian marriage. I know you and I have our struggles," I acknowledged, "but our people are hurting so much more. They need to be reminded that God—not Hollywood—created the institution of marriage and that only God's guidelines can make a marriage work." Ninfa was looking intently at me, and I continued, "You know the battles we've been through because we knew nothing about the responsibilities of husband and wife."

"Tell me about it," Ninfa smiled faintly. "We're still going through them."

"The church learns as much from our example as

---

a disciple – a student, learner, follower

[k] to disciple – to teach and bring a man to his full potential in ministry

from our teaching," I explained. "They know we haven't arrived, but they can learn even from our mistakes."

Ninfa looked down and bit her lip. "I know that's the Holy Spirit leading you," she said slowly, "because I need to learn myself." She blinked back tears, "You know, Freddie, I believe the Scripture that tells me, 'Wives, submit yourselves unto your own husbands, as unto the Lord.'[4] But I struggle to put it into practice. Lately I've come to see myself more clearly, and I don't like what I see.

"The Bible tells me that '...the husband is the head of the wife, even as Christ is the head of the church....'[5] Yet I've opposed and challenged you when I should have supported you. I've taken charge when I should have waited for your decision." She wept, "Will you forgive me?"

I held her close. "Of course I forgive you," I whispered, swallowing a big lump in my throat, "but I'm guilty too. The Word of God tells the husband that he is to love his wife 'as Christ also loved the church and gave Himself up for her.'[6] Yet I've been so busy with the ministry that I've neglected you and the kids. Can you forgive me?"

"Oh, Freddie," Ninfa cried openly, "I do love you and I do forgive you."

We embraced and wept tears of repentance. On our knees we held hands and prayed: "Thank You, Jesus, for the Holy Spirit who opens our eyes and lets us see what we are doing wrong. Forgive us for doing things

---

[4] Ephesians 5:22 (KJV)

[5] Ephesians 5:23 (KJV)

[6] Ephesians 5:25 (NASB)

our own way and help us live according to Your Word." The sweet presence of our Lord lifted our spirits and we rejoiced.

A few days later Ninfa came to me. "I've been doing some more thinking, Freddie, and I've realized that my priorities are all mixed up; I've been guilty of neglecting you and the children. I've even excused myself, saying I was too busy 'serving the Lord,' in full-time ministry. I thought that was the way to put Jesus first in my life, but I was wrong."

She sighed deeply, "It's true that Jesus is first in my life; I love Him with all my heart. But now I see that I serve Him best and honor Him, when I put your needs and the children's before the ministry." She fought back tears, *"Perdóname,*[1] Freddie."

I took her hand, "We're both to blame, Ninfa. There were times when a job needed to be done, and I pulled you away from your task as wife and mother, to have you help me in the ministry. If I had waited, I believe that Jesus would have sent someone to help me, but I was impatient."

"I'm worried, Freddie," Ninfa tried to smile. "I read in the Scriptures, 'Older women...teach the young women...to love their husbands, to love their children, to be discreet, chaste, keepers at home, good, obedient to their own husbands, that the Word of God be not blasphemed.'[7] I've been teaching them by setting the wrong example," she sobbed.

"Just ask Jesus to forgive you, Ninfa, and start doing what you know is right," I hugged her. "Get it all in balance; keep your priorities straight in your

---

[1] *Perdóname* – Forgive me.

[7] Titus 2:3-5 (NASB & KJV)

heart; take care of your obligations at home; then do what God wants in ministry. Right now, I know He wants you to share some of your experiences with the women of the church. Teach them from the Word of God and by setting a good example."

Ninfa's eyes brightened, "Oh, Freddie, I'd like to. I've seen such a need among our women. I've talked to many wives; most have the same story to tell. For years their husbands were slaves of drugs, alcohol, or whatever, and the wife was forced to be in charge of the home. Now that the husband is a Christian and wants to take on his God-ordained responsibility as head of his family, the struggle begins. The wife has been so hurt and disappointed that she doesn't trust him anymore. She's either afraid to let go of the authority, or she plain doesn't want to."

I agreed with her. "But there's another side to it, Ninfa; some of the men don't want to take the responsibility as 'head of the wife.'[8] They refuse to lead. They don't want a wife; they want a 'mother.'

"I don't want our people to be ignorant of God's Word. You teach the women and I'll teach the men. Let's go for it, Ninfa!" I smiled at her. "We ain't the greatest teachers, but let's give them our best!"

---

[8] Ephesians 5:23 (NASB)

# Chapter 10

# Battle Scars

"No weapon that is formed against you shall prosper;
And every tongue that accuses you in judgment
you will condemn.
This is the heritage of the servants of the Lord,
And their vindication is from Me," declares the Lord.

Isaiah 54:17 (NASB)

"In a month and a half our boys will finish Bible school," Ninfa snuggled close as we retired for the night. "We'll be able to go see them graduate, won't we?"

"We don't really have the money to go to El Paso and to California," I told her regretfully. "We'll just wait 'til they all come home, then have a *fiesta*ᵃ to celebrate."

Just then a gentle knock on our door interrupted our conversation. "Freddie, it's me, Gilbert. May I talk to you?"

"Can it wait 'til morning?" I asked. "We're in bed already."

"It's important," his voice sounded urgent.

I opened the door and let him in. "Hey, Freddie," he whispered, "what's going on, man?"

"What'cha talking about?" I was puzzled. "What's the problem?"

"You know that guy Raúl," he looked alarmed, "the one that went to Bible school with you and went back into drugs? He ain't your friend, Freddie. The guy

---

ᵃ *fiesta* – party

has been holding some meetings in the back dorm after you and Ninfa go to bed –"

"Yeah, I know," I cut in. "He asked permission to start an additional prayer meeting in the evening. I encouraged him and even suggested that he have it late at night, so everyone could participate."

"Prayer meetings, nothing!" Gilbert fumed. "He's been using the time to tell us that you're not qualified to be a pastor. That you're living in sin because you've been divorced and remarried. That you're stealing from the church funds, hooked on drugs, and all kinds of trash. He's been scheming behind your back to get you kicked out."

It began to dawn on me that something was really wrong; the devil had sneaked in, and this time I didn't spot him.

"I knew Raúl wasn't serving God when he came to Victory Home," I explained to Gilbert. "He'd been expelled from several drug programs, but he told me he had learned his lesson and wanted to get right with Jesus; I trusted him and took him in. I shouldn't have let him preach right away, but I remembered him as one of the most eloquent speakers in Bible school. And I thought the prayer meetings would help him get back on his feet quicker."

Gilbert shook his head. "The guy already has a group of rebels against you. They plan the first move tomorrow. You're to wake up and find yourself without anyone on your side. Raúl has promised the guys that when he becomes the new Home director, there won't be any strict rules, and they'll get paid for their work. They're going for it, Freddie. I know 'cause even I was going along with him," Gilbert confessed. "I was almost deceived, Freddie," he look frightened. "If it hadn't been for Teddy Bear, I might not be here telling you."

"Teddy Bear?" I was surprised. He was a former alcoholic in his late fifties, a quiet fellow who often dozed during Bible studies, but he loved Jesus. "What did Teddy Bear do?"

Gilbert looked embarrassed. "He was there with the rest of us in the 'prayer meeting' tonight when the plan of action against you was decided. When I got up to go to the rest room, Teddy Bear followed me. He stopped me in the hallway and said, 'Gilbert, don't do it. Don't come against Freddie; he's a man of God.'"

Gilbert fought back tears. "Teddy Bear's words jolted me from my stupor," he continued. "If anyone else had said it, I might have argued with him. But Teddy Bear is a simple, God-fearing man. He had seen what the rest of us were blind to. I knew it was God speaking to me through him." Gilbert rammed his fist into his other hand. "How close I came to joining a satanic attack against the Lord's ministry. You're the man God has placed in charge, and that's enough for me. I'm not about to go against God or His servant."

"Get the guys together right now," I told him, "and call Raúl too. We're gonna get this settled once and for all."

"They've all gone to bed, Freddie," he reminded me. "Let's wait 'til early morning."

"All right," I was hesitant, "but first thing in the morning."

I went back to bed but wasn't able to sleep. *Raúl's behavior can be explained*, I thought to myself, *but who are the rebels Gilbert is talking about?* All night long I wrestled in my soul asking the Lord to help me.

First thing in the morning, I called Raúl for a private confrontation. "I'll never understand why you've done it, Raúl, and I'm not even gonna try." I felt sadness more than anger. Raúl said nothing and I went on. "You burned all your bridges behind you. California police wants you for hot checks, several Christian centers cut you loose, yet I welcomed you into my home and heart. You repay me by turning my people against me. Man, Raúl, you're messing with souls. Don't you fear God? Tell you what, pack your things, you and your wife, and just go."

Raúl only smiled and shrugged. He left just as Gilbert came in to announce, "All the guys involved are here, Freddie."

Ready to face the kangaroo court, I walked into the office. Fifteen of the guys I had thought of as my "spiritual sons" were waiting for me. Most of them were fairly new at Victory Home. A few had completed the program and were active members of Victory Temple. Pedro, one of the church members, spoke for the group: "Freddie, we voted and decided we don't want you as our pastor. Not as our leader, or Home director, or anything. We want you out. None of us agree with the way you've been running things; we want a new pastor!"

Pedro's face was contorted with hate, and his voice was harsh. His words cut me. *Jesus*, I prayed inwardly, *what's happening? These are the guys I picked up from the streets; I taught them Your Word and I love them. ¿Qué tienen estos batos?*[b]

In stunned silence I listened, as one by one, they lashed out at me in anger, giving their reasons for not wanting me. I had used discipline to correct their behavior, and many of them had bitterly resented it.

[b] *¿Qué tienen estos batos?* – What's wrong with these guys?

Now, they intended to get even. They hurled Raúl's ugly accusations against me, and I was heartbroken. I could see that they wanted to believe the lies, wanted them to be true.

After hearing them out, I spoke. "I didn't know you had such anger in your hearts against me. I've loved you and tried my best to show you how to live the Christian life. When you were wrong, I had to correct you because I knew it would hinder your walk with Christ; I wanted you to make it. The Bible says that God uses discipline for our own good, to bring us into holiness.[1] Because I care for you, I will continue to stop you when I see you doing wrong."

I looked at each of them in turn; their faces told me nothing. I added, "If you feel I've offended you in some other way, then I ask you to forgive me." One by one I went and hugged them; some stiffened, uncomfortable at my embrace. They had rejected all I had said.

I squared my shoulders and stood my ground. "Because I'm not guilty of your accusations, I'm not stepping down. I'm your pastor and your Home director and that's final. I still love you, and you're welcome to stay. You decide for yourselves what you want to do. Now let's pray, and afterwards, you're dismissed." During the prayer I felt the undercurrent of hostility. The battle wasn't over yet.

The seriousness of the situation became even more apparent that Friday in church. Our congregation numbered 150 adults, but only 100 showed up for worship service. "Raúl has been visiting our church members during the day," Ninfa told me afterwards. "A few have called to let us know the filth he's been

---

[1] Hebrews 12:10 (NASB)

telling them."

Sunday morning, only seventy people came to church, and I noted sadly that even our head usher, David Pérez, was absent. I had a sickening feeling of complete rejection. Never, since coming to Jesus, had Ninfa and I felt so alone.

That afternoon, David Pérez stormed into our bedroom. "Freddie!" He gave me a bear hug, "I didn't know! I just heard and rushed over here." With tears in his eyes, he added, "You're my pastor, Freddie; I'm with you."

His wife had hurled herself past me and held Ninfa in a tight embrace. They were weeping in each other's arms.

"When I didn't see you at church, I thought you'd gone over to their side," I confessed to David.

"No, Freddie," he shook his head, "I've been working the night shift these past weeks. That's the only reason I haven't been in church."

David's support was a comfort, but the gnawing pain in my stomach returned when that same Sunday evening the congregation had dwindled to fifty. Most of the people greeted Ninfa and me stiffly, formally, almost as if we were strangers. I could sense their distrust, and I felt betrayed. A thought was nagging in the back of my mind: *It's all over, Freddie. Pack up your things and leave. Your ministry with the drug addicts is over.*

Night after night I stayed awake, unable to sleep. I felt drained, physically exhausted, and my head had been aching for days. *It can't be any clearer than this*, I finally concluded. *These people don't want me here.*

"Let's just pack our bags and leave," I told Ninfa. "They want Victory Home and Victory Temple church?

Well, let them have it. We can start a new work for the Lord in some other city."

"No!" Ninfa's voice jolted me. "We're not leaving!" She put her hands on her hips and faced me defiantly.

I exploded, "Why can't you ever agree with anything I say? You've always got to argue. I'll tell you what, Ninfa, you want to stay? Fine. I'm leaving!"

"No, you're not!" she erupted. "You know why you're not leaving? 'Cause you're not a quitter." Her eyes challenged me. "Even as a junkie you were never a quitter, and you're not gonna quit now that you're a minister of the gospel! You'd never be able to face yourself in the mirror."

I slumped on the edge of the bed and buried my face in my hands. I couldn't deny the reality of her words–I had to stay. All the strength I'd summoned up to say I was leaving left me, and I fell to my knees in prayer. Hot tears stung my eyes. "It hurts, Lord," I whispered in anguish. "It hurts to see people that I've helped turn around and stab us. It hurts to stay where I'm not wanted, but a pastor doesn't leave his flock. I'll stay, Jesus, I'll stay."

Ninfa knelt with me and we embraced, crying in each other's arms. We still weren't prepared for the heartaches ahead.

Monday morning at six a.m. Ninfa awakened me, "Josie's got a very bad headache, Freddie. May I keep her home from school for the day, so I can watch over her?"

"Let her stay in bed," I agreed. "Drop everything else and tend to her."

Close to noon I walked into the living room just in time to see Juan Miguel Rivera step in the front door. *He's supposed to be in Bible school*, the thought flashed through my head. *What's he doing here?* I sought out his eyes. *Does he know what's going on? Is he for or against me?* I didn't know what to expect anymore.

Juan smiled and grasped my hand, "Before you say anything, I want you to know I've heard the rumors; I don't believe them. I'm on your side."

"Juan–" I tried to explain.

"I don't want to hear it," he repeated. "I'm with you and that's final. I'm just gonna go drop Raider off at his home, and I'll be back. I'm staying to help."

I had no time to reflect on what he had said; the minute he walked out, I heard Josie scream in terror. I rushed into the bedroom to find her lying unconscious on the floor. Ninfa was trying to awaken her.

"What's wrong?!" I yelled.

"I don't know!" Ninfa was crying. "She just fainted."

"Father, in the name of Jesus, heal my daughter," I prayed. "Touch her in Jesus' name."

Josie was starting to come around. She sobbed in pain, "My eyes, Daddy! I can't see!"

My heart sank. "Get up, Josie," I tried to pull her up from the floor. "Get up."

"I can't," she wept. "My legs–I have no strength. And my head, Daddy, it feels like it's being split open." She clung to me. One of the guys walked into the bedroom just in time to help me pick her up and place her on the bed. Ninfa had dashed out of the room and returned with a wet cloth. She placed it over Josie's forehead. Josie's body was limp, but thank God, her eyesight had returned. After a while she fell asleep.

"Take her to the doctor," I told Ninfa. "Find out what's wrong."

"But...we don't have money," she looked distressed. "What do I tell them at the hospital?"

"Tell them that we'll take care of the bill in payments; just take her!"

An hour and a half later, Ninfa phoned from the hospital. "Josie's been admitted. The doctors said the symptoms she's been having are caused by severe migraine headaches. They've already knocked her out with Valium to get her to rest. But Josie wants me to stay the night with her."

"You do that," I urged her. "Don't worry about Paul; I'll take care of him. Tell Josie I love her and that we're praying for Jesus to heal her."

\*　　　　\*　　　　\*

Long before dawn Tuesday morning, heavy thumping on the door awakened me. "Hey, Freddie!" a familiar voice rang out, "It's me—Manuel!...Zertuche!"

"Manuel?" I checked the clock. "It's 2:34 a.m.!" I ran to open the door. Outside stood the rest of our Bible-school students.

"We heard," Juan Garza's hand clasped mine, "and we came to see how we can help."

They each hugged me and gripped my hand. Their love and compassion soothed my inward pain. "How did you guys hear all the way to California?"

"This dude called me," Manuel pointed to Juan Rivera.

"And how did you hear about it in El Paso?" I turned to Juan Rivera.

"Oh, you know," he grinned, "through the grapevine." They all roared with laughter and I joined in. It seemed like an eternity since I'd really laughed, and it felt good.

"How did you guys get the money to come?"

"No problem," Juan Rivera boasted. "El Paso is not that far. The Bible-school superintendent lent me the money for gas."

Juan Garza cleared his throat. "We drove the school van from California. When I explained to our principal why we needed to be with you, he not only lent us the van but his credit card to get here."

"We're ready!" Manuel announced. "Just tell us how we can help."

They were full of energy, and their eyes shone with faith and courage. Somehow I felt like a wounded soldier under enemy attack seeing the Marines land with reinforcements. "Catch some sleep," I told them. "You still have a good three hours left before sun-up. We'll talk after you've rested."

All day Tuesday, God used our Bible-school students to bless my weary soul. We laughed, prayed, and worshipped Jesus together. "I don't know if anyone will show up in church tomorrow," I warned them, "but you guys be there to take charge of the worship service. You know what to do."

\*        \*        \*

Wednesday afternoon Gilbert and Lee went with me to pray at the church earlier than usual. For the first time in over a week, I was at peace. "I feel the presence of the Lord so strong," I told them, "that I'm not afraid of whatever happens anymore. If no one shows up, we'll preach to the empty benches and each other." Gilbert's laughter echoed in the empty church.

When the service began, only thirty people were there. Against the back wall stood Pedro and a few of his followers, smiling in triumph.

Our Bible-school students, under the leading of the Holy Spirit, sprang into action with the ease and precision of a drill team. They directed the song service, gave testimonies, and preached the sermon.

Before church was dismissed, I got up and spoke to my congregation. "All of you are aware of what's been going on. You've been told that I'm living in sin. I have no way of really proving my innocence, but I can tell you that I'm not guilty of doing what I've been accused of. You can believe what you want, but get this through your heads: God has placed me as your pastor. You did not hire me, so you can't fire me."

\*　　　　\*　　　　\*

Ninfa brought Josie home from the hospital Thursday, completely recovered. She explained what had happened during the past four days: "The doctors didn't know what was causing the migraine headaches. They just kept giving her drugs, morning, noon, and night: Valium, Darvon, and phenobarbital. I knew they weren't curing the problem, so each time Josie fell asleep, I laid hands on her and prayed. I asked Jesus to heal her.

"Josie woke up Wednesday morning still in pain. When a church member came to visit and began talking about all the church problems, Josie started to yell, 'I hate them! I hate them all! I hate them!' It frightened me, Freddie. I took Josie in my arms and tried to calm her. When I reminded her, 'Hate is not from God, *mi hija,*c' she broke down and started sobbing. Out gushed all she had secretly held in her

---

c *mi hija* – my daughter

heart."

Ninfa's eyes were moist, "Do you realize that Raúl and his wife tried to talk our Josie into leaving with them?"

"They what?" I couldn't believe my ears.

"They told her that you and I didn't really appreciate her singing talent, but if she left with them, they would give her the opportunity to minister in song in different churches. They promised to give her all the offering, and they even guaranteed she'd get the private bedroom we never bothered to get her."

I was speechless. Ninfa's face was somber. "And that's not all," she sighed heavily. "Josie and Paul have been ridiculed openly in children's church. The kids have been saying what they hear at home–'My mom and dad say that your mom and dad live in sin.'

"Paul is eight years old," Ninfa's lips trembled. "Josie is not even twelve. How can people be so mean, getting back at us by hurting our children?" she stifled a sob. "Josie had nowhere to hide, Freddie. Even in school, her teacher called her aside and told her that he'd heard her mom and dad were having trouble at church."

"How come she never told us?" I felt a heaviness inside. "Why didn't she let us know?"

Ninfa could no longer hold back her tears, "Josie saw all the pain you and I were being put through, and she didn't want us to hurt anymore. She tried to protect us, Freddie, and kept it all inside–that's what caused the migraine headaches."

Ninfa touched my arm, "But the Lord did a miracle in our daughter. The moment Josie confessed the anger, and asked Jesus to forgive her and help her to love all those people that hurt us, she was healed instantly. The migraine headaches left and never came back. The doctors checked her. They couldn't find anything wrong and released her."

I said nothing, and we walked over to the bedroom. My heart went out to Josie when I saw her, thin and pale on the bed. *"Mi hija,"* I enfolded her in my arms and kissed her, "never carry the burdens of life on your own shoulders. Give them over to Jesus."

"I know, Dad," she kissed me and then Ninfa. "I love you both."

That night we thanked the Lord for healing our daughter and for keeping our family together through the storm.

\*　　　　\*　　　　\*

Early Friday morning the phone rang. It was Raider. "Freddie, can you make time to see me today? It's very important."

"Come on over," I told him. "I'll be waiting."

When he arrived, his face was grim. "I don't even know how to begin, Freddie, other than to come straight out and say it. A few guys from the church called me to a private meeting. They want me to be their pastor. It was tempting, Freddie, but I knew it wasn't Jesus. I rebuked them and warned them of God's judgment. I figure if they treat you, their spiritual father, like that, what can I expect? Man, I don't want a bunch of rebels with me. What do I do?"

"Most of these guys aren't rebels," I counselled Raider. "They're victims of a satanic lie. Raúl poisoned their minds. They saw him well mannered, well dressed, and with a fantastic memory for Scriptures; so they fell for it. But if you do what I tell you,

Raider, Jesus will still be glorified."

"I'll do whatever you say, Freddie," he was attentive.

"Go back and tell the group that you'll pastor them, but that the name of the church is to be Victory Chapel."

Raider's eyes widened with amazement and I chuckled. "You'll still be under the Victory Outreach umbrella," I assured him, "but this way, you'll have your own church, and they'll have their new pastor. Satan's plan is to destroy this ministry," I reminded him, "but in God's perfect wisdom, instead of one church, we'll have two."

\*　　　　\*　　　　\*

Pastor Sonny Arguinzoni, my spiritual father, arrived with Pastor Ruben Reyna, from Los Angeles that afternoon. When Sonny saw me, he smiled, embraced me, and in his Puerto Rican accent asked, "*¿Cómo está?*–How are you?–You okay?"

"All I can say is that I'm not guilty," I struggled to swallow the lump in my throat.

He gave me another warm hug. "I believe you, Freddie, and I will always stand by you." I felt God's love for me in Sonny's words, and I could no longer hold back the tears. With his hand on my shoulder, Sonny began to pray in tongues. The sweet presence of the Holy Spirit filled the entire room.

"Look at you, Freddie," Sonny's voice was kind. "You're all broken inside, but that's the kind of man God will use. You can't see it right now because you're hurting, but you'll be more sensitive than ever to the moving of the Holy Spirit in your life." Sonny was getting excited. "What I see happening is that in the midst of this storm, the Holy Spirit is going to sift the wheat from the chaff within your church. He's gonna clean house. Then an overwhelming anointing will come upon your life and upon those brethren who are faithful." He lifted his hands and shouted, "Hallelujah! This ministry is going to grow, Freddie!"

The evening worship service drew a full house—all wanting to hear what Pastor Sonny had to say.

"I've come to speak what God has laid on my heart," he told the congregation. "God has warned us in His Word: 'Do not touch My anointed ones....'[2] Be careful how you speak of God's servant. Freddie is the man God has chosen for this work in this city. If, in ignorance or anger, you spoke harshly against your pastor but are now willing to repent, God is willing to forgive. If you choose to continue in your stubborn rebellion, I'm going to tell you what's going to happen to you.

"Number One: Some of you will walk away from God, perhaps never to return.

"Number Two: Others will become church tramps, going from church to church, never establishing roots for Christian growth anywhere.

"Number Three: Still others will leave and come back broken by the circumstances in their lives.

"Come here, Freddie," he beckoned me. "You too, Ninfa." Putting one arm around my shoulders and the other around Ninfa's, he confronted the people. "Listen carefully. I'm flying back to California tomorrow morning. If you don't want your pastor and his wife, I'll take them with me. In Los Angeles there's a lot of people who love them and want them back. Just

---

[2] 1 Chronicles 16:22 (NASB)

let me know, and I'll take them with me right now."

Church members began making their way to the altar, some weeping softly, others out loud, calling upon Jesus to forgive them. One by one they came up to us, expressing their love. All except Pedro and a few of his followers. They walked out of Victory Temple and never returned.

*         *         *

Our Bible-school students headed back that weekend to finish their last three weeks of school. David Pérez came by to see me later that week. "Satan sure tried hard to destroy this ministry, right, Freddie?"

"He threw his best shot," I agreed. "He used the ex-drug addicts I had picked up from the streets to hurt me so I'd get angry and stop loving them. If I had allowed anger and hatred in my heart, my ministry to the drug addict would have been over. But thank God that the devil's plan backfired. You see, David, it's not Freddie's love, *it's God's love* in my life that draws the drug addict to Christ."

"Thank You, Jesus!" David grinned.

"That's right," I was excited, "and we're not gonna take it sitting down; we're fighting right back. Juan Rivera has already set up the date and place for a city-wide presentation of *The Junkie*, a six-scene drama portraying the life of the addict. Harold Velásquez, and his gospel group, 'The Latinos,' will minister in music–so get your ushers ready, David."

"Amen!" David had caught my enthusiasm. "Amen!" he shouted.

"We're gonna blow it up big," I outlined our plan.

"We'll put up posters at every drug connection, every beer joint–any place where people are hurting. And we're gonna give away a '45' recording with Ninfa's testimony on one side and mine on the other to everyone who comes. It's our way of saying Jesus loves them; He has the power to change lives and keep those that want to be kept.

"We're involved in spiritual warfare, David, and there's no turning back. In Jesus' name there's no foe that can defeat us. We're going forward; we're gonna take Texas for Jesus!"

# Chapter 11

# Go Therefore and Make Disciples

Go therefore and make disciples of all the nations,
baptizing them in the name of the Father
and the Son and the Holy Spirit.

Matthew 28:19 (NASB)

"I graduated with high honors, Freddie!" Juan
Garza proudly showed us his diploma.

"Didn't you tell me you were too dumb to make it in
Bible school?" I teased him.

"Amen, Pastor Freddie," Juan Garza's smile broadened, "but Jesus helped me."

By the end of the week, all our graduates had
arrived. "What have you guys decided to do, now that
you've finished school?" I asked them.

"I don't know about the other guys," Juan Rivera
replied quickly, "but I know the Lord wants me to stay
and help you in the church."

"That goes for me too," Manuel Zertuche joined in.
"We'll go to work in whatever area of the ministry you
need us the most."

"In that case," I turned to Juan Rivera, "I'll disciple[a] you as my co-pastor. You, Manuel, can take over
as Victory Home director so I can be free to minister

---

a disciple – a student, learner, follower

[a] to disciple – to teach and bring a man to his full potential in
ministry

in the county jail and prisons."

"I'm ready!" Manuel agreed. "Let's go for it."

"Freddie," Juan Garza was excited, "I'm thinking of going back to my hometown. No one's taken the gospel to those on the streets of Laredo, Texas. That city needs a Victory Temple church and a Home."

"Great!" I shouted. "Thank You, Jesus."

"I'm looking for a building here in San Antonio," Raider grinned. "We'll soon have a Victory Chapel on the south side."

I rejoiced in my heart. "Didn't I tell you from the start that God was going to use your lives to do His work, that one day we would plant Victory churches and Victory Homes all over Texas? Well, we're seeing the start of that vision come true."

"*¡Gloria a Dios!*—Glory to God!" they cheered. "Hallelujah!"

"But don't ever forget," I cautioned, "God wants us in the *barrios*[b] reaching the poor people. Open up your homes to them and help meet their needs. Start your Bible studies there. Win people to Christ, and begin having worship services at home; then look for a storefront building to hold your church services in. Don't wait 'til you have a church building to start a ministry. Start at home."

I was excited to see that our guys had caught the vision of launching out to other cities, but there was something else just as important that I had to share. "We need to talk about a problem that keeps increasing as new guys come in. Many of them want to be preachers or Bible teachers but can't afford to go to Bible school.

---

[b] *barrios* – neighborhoods

"I've wrestled in prayer about this for a long time, and the Lord has impressed on me that I, as their pastor, and you, as their spiritual leaders, are responsible for training our own future ministers. It would be easier to raise the money to send them to Bible school, but I've finally come to accept that this is not what God wants us to do."

The guys were silent, but I had their undivided attention. "The Word of God says that Jesus gave the church some to be apostles, prophets, evangelists, pastors, and teachers. They in turn would 'prepare God's people for works of service, so that the body of Christ may be built up.'[1] Therefore, from now on, we disciple our own church leaders, pastors, teachers, and so on."

"Does that mean no more sending our guys to Bible school at all?" Juan Rivera looked baffled.

"That's right," I stated. "But don't get me wrong, praise God for Bible schools. I commend them for taking over the task that many of us pastors have neglected to do."

The guys were listening intently. I knew they were weighing my words in the light of the Scriptures. "Here in Victory Outreach of Texas, we will not continue to ignore the responsibility of discipling our own men for ministry," I declared, "for it is from within the church that the pastors, teachers, and evangelists should be reproduced."

"What about José Luis Flores, Marcos Gonzales, and Danny Ibarra who are still in Bible school?" Juan Garza injected. "What do we do about them?"

"They should complete their studies," I replied.

---

[1] Ephesians 4:11-12 (NIV)

"But after these graduate—no more."

The guys looked at each other. "How are we going to disciple men for ministry?" Manuel broke the silence.

"How did Jesus do it?" I asked. "I'll tell you how He did it; Jesus spent hours with His disciples. He taught them and they learned by watching Him. Everything Jesus did, His disciples saw how He did it and followed His example. They prayed and fasted because He prayed and fasted; they preached in the streets because He preached in the streets. His disciples had on-the-job training of street preaching, teaching, personal witnessing, counselling, and living the Christian life. When His disciples were ready, Jesus told them: 'Go therefore and make disciples....'[2] That's how we'll do it.

"Jesus said that every disciple 'who is fully trained will be like his teacher.'[3] The Apostle Paul picked up discipling from Jesus. He wrote to the Corinthian church, 'Be imitators of me, just as I also am of Christ.'[4] Everywhere he went, Paul planted churches and discipled men as pastors to care for the flock. He told his disciple Timothy, 'And the things which you have heard from me...these entrust to faithful men, who will be able to teach others also.'[5] Jesus has commanded us to make disciples who will go out and reproduce disciples, who in turn will reproduce disciples, and so on, 'til the Lord returns."

"That's some heavy teaching," Manuel Zertuche sighed, "but it's Bible, Freddie."

---

[2] Matthew 28:19 (NASB)

[3] Luke 6:40 (NIV)

[4] 1 Corinthians 11:1 (NASB)

[5] 2 Timothy 2:2 (NASB)

"That's right," the guys echoed all around. "Amen! Amen!"

"Now, I'm going to ask you a question, Manuel," I turned to him. "How did I disciple you? It was not a structured thing; it was a father and son relationship. When you had a question or a doubt, you came to me. I took time out to teach you on a man-to-man basis. Remember how we studied the Bible together, over coffee, under a tree? We even talked about it in the car.

"Then I got you involved in doing what you'd been taught. Remember in the beginning when I taught you street witnessing? We acted it out first in the Home; then I took you to Guadalupe Street, and I showed you by example how to do it. Then it was your turn to witness." They laughed and nodded.

I pointed to Juan Garza, "Remember the Christmas rallies in the streets downtown? I taught you first what we were going to do, and then we went and did it. I got you involved in doing rallies, testifying, and preaching.

"And you," I turned to Juan Rivera, "remember when I taught you how to testify in the public schools? I took you along to watch me first; then you gave your testimony. When you had learned how to give the presentation and counsel the students, I stepped back and let you take over.

"We didn't call it 'discipling' back then, but that's what we were doing. I discipled you like a father teaching his sons from the first day you came to Victory Home, and you're living proof that it works."

"Amen," they looked at each other and nodded, "amen!"

"The Apostle Paul called himself a 'father' to his

disciples," I continued. "He wrote to the church: 'For if you were to have countless tutors in Christ, yet you would not have many fathers; for in Christ Jesus I became your father through the gospel. I exhort you therefore, be imitators of me.'[6]

"There are plenty of preachers and teachers, but what the church needs is more 'spiritual fathers,'" I emphasized. "The church is a family. Our disciples are our spiritual sons. In fact," I smiled, "while you've been away at school, I've discipled your younger 'brothers.' I taught them on a man-to-man basis and provided them the tools they needed for ministry. Pancho is ready to pastor a Victory church on the east side!"

The guys looked surprised, and I added, "Pancho is as qualified as any Bible-school graduate. During the day he and the others had on-the-job training; in the evening they studied the Bible commentaries and books I assigned for them. They wrote book reports and learned to do sermon outlines. They listened to teaching tapes and wrote summaries and reports on them, and I was always available when they needed me."

I grinned, "Wait 'til you see the library of books and tapes I'm putting together: Bible commentaries; dictionaries; books and tapes on prayer, Christian doctrine, evangelism, discipling, follow-up, Christian family, church growth—any subject related to Christian growth and ministry. I'm always on the lookout for new study material that may be useful to my disciples."

"I've got a question," Manuel spoke up. "Do these guys have to buy their own books and tapes, Freddie?"

---

[6] 1 Corinthians 4:15,16 (NASB)

"No," I shook my head. "They don't have the money. This is a father and son relationship. Would you charge your son for the school books you buy for him? Or for anything else he needs in growing up? No! A father provides for his son.

"I provide for my disciples the books, the tapes, the pencils, notebooks, even the tape recorder, if they don't have one. You'll get them too, and—you'll be turning in some book reports."

"Man, Freddie," Manuel laughed and shook his head, "we thought we had graduated from Bible school; now you're telling us we've just started learning!"

I laughed at the expression on their faces, "That's the idea. We ain't none of us arrived; we're never through learning. I never stop studying. What I learn and what I find in the Bible or in Christian books and tapes, I'll pass on to my disciples. You, in turn, pass it on to yours.

"But listen. You're not gonna produce disciples just by handing out books and tapes—DISCIPLESHIP AND DISCIPLING IS CAUGHT, NOT TAUGHT. Discipleship is the state of being a student. *How will your disciple catch 'discipleship' unless he sees you being a 'learner' yourself.* The same works for discipling; your men won't make disciples unless they see you discipling. They see you doing it and they catch it.

"Can you see where I'm coming from?" I went on. "If you look around, you'll see that you've already been discipling. You've always got guys hanging around, watching, listening, and doing what you're doing."

The guys were grinning and nodding their heads.

"One of the keys to making disciples is involvement," I emphasized. "Your disciple won't catch it unless you get him involved in evangelism, discipling, and follow-up on new Christians. You reach people for Christ through evangelism; you reproduce leaders through discipling; you nurture the people in their relationship with Christ and the church through follow-up. Your disciple has to be involved in all these areas—and produce results—before he's ready to be launched out."

"But, Freddie," Juan Garza spoke up, "how long does it take to get a man ready?"

"That depends on the individual," I replied. "But on the average you teach a man the basics of the Christian life for six months, how to make it as a Christian. You prepare him so he can disciple another man in the basics, who will disciple another man in the basics and so on. But if he feels the calling to be a pastor, you disciple him for two years and then launch him out.

"Just be careful," I cautioned them. "ALL THE HOURS YOU SPEND TRAINING YOUR DISCIPLES AND ALL THE BOOKS AND TAPES YOU GIVE THEM ARE USELESS IF YOU AND YOUR DISCIPLES DON'T HAVE A LIFE OF PRAYER AND FASTING.

"Start each day with your disciple in prayer, at least for an hour. Fast at least one day of the week. Jesus, the Son of God, lived a life of prayer and fasting, and He left the example for us to follow. We are His disciples, but He can't disciple us unless we spend time with Him in prayer.

"But be careful to keep this in mind: Disciples should be recruited to Jesus, not to Freddie, or Manuel, or Juan. We are their spiritual fathers, but a good father doesn't dominate his son." I laughed, "A good father even hopes that his son will turn out better than himself. Some of you guys are turning out better than me, and when I see it, I'm pleased. That was my intention in the first place."

They smiled and I added, "Of course, I wouldn't want you to get puffed up like a frog and proud of yourself; that's why the guys who are being discipled to pastor are responsible for cleaning the church as well. They give a beautiful sermon and everybody praises them, and then they go scrub the bathrooms. It keeps them in balance." They cheered and roared with laughter. They'd all had their turns on the "clean-up committee."

When they quieted down, I turned to Juan Garza. "Before you get established in Laredo, I want your wife to start coming to the office. I want Ninfa to disciple her in bookkeeping and filing, how to write thank-you letters and answer prison correspondence, and all the paper work that is needed to help the ministry function."

"Sounds good, Freddie," Juan Garza looked pleased.

Manuel shouted, "Praise God! We're gonna do it, Freddie; we're gonna make disciples for Jesus!"

"Amen!" they all joined in. "¡Gloria a Dios!"

I lifted up my hands, "Let's just take time to worship Jesus."

Immediately the sound of our voices rose in one accord, praying and praising God. We sensed the presence of the Holy Spirit, and a gentle hush spread throughout the room. One of the guys began to sing, "He is Lord, He is Lord...He is risen from the dead and He is Lord." Soon everyone had joined him in singing to God.

A sense of awe and gratitude welled up in me. "Thank You, Heavenly Father, thank You for opening up our understanding," I prayed.

\* \* \*

We had been able to complete another dorm in the back of Victory Home so that we had thirty beds for men and ten for women. However, the average population of the Home was more often fifty with some winter months bringing in as many as sixty. They slept on the floor of every room, but our policy was never to turn anyone away.

We had added a bathroom with two showers, two toilets, and two lavatories. Manuel Zertuche was a carpenter by trade. Out of thick plywood he built handmade wardrobes and footlockers for each bunk in the dorms. As they were completed, Jose Luis painted them. Mama and Ninfa made individual patchwork quilts for each bunk from donated blankets and clothing. By most standards our facilities were still primitive, but to our guys, it was home.

With Manuel in charge of Victory Home, Ninfa, the children, and I moved back to our little house on 658 N. San Eduardo Street. It had been in use by the families of some of the guys in our program but now was vacant.

Luis Salazar, a young Peruvian we nicknamed Luis "Perú," moved in with us, but still we had more privacy now than at Victory Home. Our children needed it, and there was an added reason–Ninfa was pregnant. The baby was due in November, and we were all looking forward to "his" arrival.

I decided to take with us my office work, files, and

equipment. "That way," I explained to Ninfa, "I can work at home, and I won't miss out on seeing our kids grow up." Smiling at my own thought I added, "I want to have memories of when Paul starts noticing girls. And I gotta keep my eye on Josie, 'cause she's blooming into a beautiful young lady."

"I love the voice God has given our daughter," Ninfa's eyes shone, "and I pray she will use it to sing for Jesus all the days of her life."

I nodded. "I believe God wants Josie to record an album someday," I told Ninfa. "She's got it in her. But I want you to concentrate on helping her become the woman she was created to be. She loves God and she prays and reads her Bible. But teach her also the art of cooking and homemaking so that one day she'll be a godly wife and mother."

"Mama already taught her how to make *tortillas*,[c]" Ninfa chuckled.

"Thank You, Jesus," I was pleased. "Thank You, Jesus."

Late that night my son's voice broke into my prayer, "Dad." Paul was standing in the doorway shyly motioning for me to come. I went to him, and he looked carefully both ways making sure no one was listening. "I'd like to learn to play the piano," he whispered.

I put my arms around him, "Do you believe that if we ask Jesus to teach you how to play the piano, He'll do it?" With his child-like trust, he nodded. I took his small hands in mine and prayed, "Father, in the name of Jesus, give Paul the ability to learn how to play the piano that he may use his talent to Your glory alone."

---

[c] *tortilla* – a thin, unleavened pancake characteristic of Mexican cookery

"Amen," Paul agreed.

When Mama heard about Paul's desire, she felt moved by God to buy him a studio piano. Right away Paul began practicing several hours a day, picking up tunes by ear. There was no doubt that God had gifted him.

\*     \*     \*

Early in July, I received an exciting phone call and quickly called a meeting of the guys. "We're doing a city-wide crusade with David Wilkerson in December!" I announced.

"David Wilkerson?" Juan Rivera was taken by surprise. "Isn't he the preacher in *The Cross and the Switchblade*?"

"That's him," I smiled. "He's the man God used to take the gospel of Jesus Christ to the junkies on the streets of New York. He's heard about our work and is interested in helping us reach the addicts in San Antonio. He's gonna be the main speaker in our December crusade."

"Thank You, Jesus!" the guys cheered and applauded.

"You want me to get you the Municipal Auditorium?" Juan Rivera volunteered.

"Right!" I agreed, "and get David Pérez, I wanna talk with him." David, an aircraft mechanic at Kelly Air Force Base, had come to know Jesus as his Savior at Victory Temple. For the past two years, I had been discipling him. He was head usher, discipling our twelve ushers for leadership in the church.

These men were trained in organizing and running all the behind-the-scene activities connected with the church functions and *barrio* rallies. They were also discipled in evangelism and in counselling those who came forward to accept Christ.

Our six usherettes were women discipled to be part of the welcoming committee, to counsel and lead other women to Christ, and to pray with them at the altar.

David discipled all of them with the love and compassion of a father for his children. He brought their families together with his for Bible studies and fellowship. They were a highly motivated team with disciples of their own.

David was on fire for Jesus, and I knew he would be excited about the David Wilkerson crusade. He'd get his troops ready. When he came to my house that evening, he had already heard the news and was jumping with enthusiasm. "You know what to do," I told him. "Get the ushers and usherettes prepared. This will be big."

"Got you covered," he grinned. "And they've got their uniforms ready. The guys have their black pants, red shirts, red berets; the girls have their white gloves and long, red dresses. The works."

Brother Lee was in the kitchen, listening, and stuck his head through the doorway, "Hey, Freddie, how come it's red shirts, red berets, and red dresses–red everything?"

"So people will ask just like you did now," I laughed. "And we get a chance to tell them that red symbolizes the blood of Jesus shed on Calvary. The Bible says that '...the blood of Jesus Christ...cleanseth us from all sin.'[7] The power is in the blood of Jesus!"

---

[7] 1 John 1:7 (KJV)

"*Es todo*–Right on!" Lee raised his hands and returned to the kitchen. We could hear him yelling, "Thank You, Jesus!"

We had four months to prepare. David would need to train more ushers and usherettes for the big event. "It's gonna be a night to remember, Freddie," David smiled as he headed for the door. "We'll be ready when it comes."

\*         \*         \*

One evening as we finished supper, Luis "Perú" turned to me, "Could you make time to talk to me a little later?"

"Why not now?" I got up. "Let's go for a ride." I drove towards Woodlawn Lake where it would be quiet. "What's on your mind?"

"I want you to disciple me for full-time ministry, Freddie," Luis was serious.

"If you want me to disciple you," I advised him, "I'm gonna expect four things from you: submission, obedience, commitment, and loyalty.[8] Now, you tell me if you're willing to go along with these conditions. If not, I'll understand, and we'll continue just the way we've been doing it."

"I've seen how you work with your disciples, Freddie," he nodded, "and I know that you're strict. But I see God using their lives, and I don't want to be left out."

"There's one more thing," I warned him. "You're a young man, and I ask that you give me one year without having a sweetheart. I'm not trying to be dictatorial, but I know from years of experience in working

---

[8] Luke 9:23 (NASB)

with my disciples that a girl friend will sidetrack them from seeking the Lord and studying the Word. Instead of praying, they'll be talking on the phone; instead of studying, they'll be going out on a date. And that first year of training can make the difference in whether or not you succeed in your ministry."

Luis smiled sheepishly, "I'm not looking for a sweetheart, Freddie, not now anyway. I really want you to teach me."

"I don't want you to get me wrong, Luis," I chuckled. "You know I believe in marriage. In fact, one of the qualifications for pastors in the Bible is that he be '...the husband of one wife...one who manages his own household well....'[9] You see, Luis, God compares the responsibility of a pastor to that of a husband and father. Through marriage you learn to 'pastor' your wife and household first; then you are ready to pastor His church. You know I've never launched out a guy to open up a ministry unless he is married. But there's enough time in your second year to start thinking about that. The Lord will send you the right girl."

Luis smiled, "Thank you, Freddie. When do we start?"

It was my turn to smile. "Why do you think I've had you teach the fifteen Bible-study lessons to new guys coming into the church? And put you in charge of the children's church and the tape and film ministry? Every time I've taken you along on rides, I've been planting the vision of what God has called us to do. I started discipling you a long time ago."

He looked amazed and glad. I continued, "Tell you

---

[9] 1 Timothy 3:2,4 (NASB)

what, Luis, I'm gonna give you a book or teaching tapes to do a written report on. Whenever you're done, I'll start you with another book or tapes. From now on, I want you to sit and listen to the conversations or counsel that I give to any one of my leaders. Pay attention—get all you can, and 'can' all you get—learn from their victories and failures. Any questions you have, don't be afraid to ask at any time."

"Thank You, Jesus," Luis squared his shoulders and smiled. "Thank you, Freddie."

Every morning, the leaders in the different areas of the ministry came to my home with their disciples for prayer, then coffee and breakfast. We talked about what they were doing and their plans for the day. When they made mistakes, I corrected them with Scripture and encouraged them.

Then each leader took his disciple aside—to a corner of the house, on the porch, or in the yard—for Bible teaching before heading out to their different ministries.

Daily I took time to meet with my own disciples without their disciples. We discussed the special problems and needs of our people, the difficult issues of life and death that confronted us as we ministered. I taught from the Scriptures how to apply the healing message of Jesus Christ to the suffering world around us.

\*       \*       \*

The Wilkerson Crusade was coming closer. We had rented the Municipal Auditorium, and two weeks before the big event 8,000 posters went up all over the city. Newspapers, radio, and television advertised the crusade a week ahead; three days before, we flooded the city with 50,000 flyers.

In the midst of the preparations, Ninfa gave birth to our son Jubal, and I asked David Wilkerson to dedicate him to the Lord during the crusade.

Pastor Sonny had flown in from Los Angeles. He and I would testify first; then Dallas Holm would sing, and Brother David Wilkerson would preach.

More than 4,000 people filled the Municipal Auditorium, and I watched as David Pérez supervised his ushers and usherettes. David had drilled them for weeks in advance, and they moved with precision directing the large crowd. The red dresses of the girls and the red shirts and berets of the guys were easily visible in the throng of people. They were matched by arrangements of bright red carnations on each side of the stage.

David Wilkerson stepped to the microphone, and I called Ninfa to join us on the platform with Jubal. Brother Dave took our infant son in his arms and prayed:

"Lord Jesus, this is scriptural: to return our children to You, to be given and blessed. We thank You, Lord, for blessing these parents. Lord, this child could have been born a drug addict. Hundreds of children are born as drug addicts through the blood stream of their mothers. They cry as they withdraw from drugs, and oh, Lord, this is something his parents have thought about. Without Jesus, this child could've been born a junkie, and now, Lord, what a difference Jesus makes! Thank You, Lord, for this little child. We pray the prayer You told us to pray. I pray, therefore, the Lord of the

Harvest, that He would send forth laborers unto His vineyard. And I take Jubal in my arms and give him to You again, and say, Lord, send him into Your harvest field. His parents give him to You, right now. Amen."

David Wilkerson's sermon went straight to the heart of the audience. When Brother Dave challenged the crowd to accept Jesus as their Savior, many strung-out[d] junkies came forward. In all, over 600 people responded to the invitation.

I had invited pastors from other denominations in the city to attend the crusade with counsellors from their own congregations. They came to the altar to pray with the converts and invite them to join their churches. Several of the junkies who accepted Christ went to Pancho's church, others went to Raider's, and the rest came with us to Victory Home.

\*         \*         \*

Six months later, our last three guys were graduating from Bible school. José Luis Flores was planning to go help Juan Garza in Laredo, Texas. Marcos Gonzales would be leaving for Austin, Texas, to start a Victory Home and Victory church there. Danny Ibarra had decided to return to San Antonio after graduation. He had already sold his furniture and was packed and ready to leave.

"Freddie," he called me from El Paso, "all the students' pastors will be coming to the graduation. I'd sure like you to be present."

When I arrived in El Paso, Danny took me on a tour

---

[d] strung-out – addicted for a long time

of the *barrios*. He kept talking about the need for a Victory Home and church in the city. I agreed but said nothing. I knew his struggle—but it was a decision he'd have to make alone. On the way to the graduation, Danny finally acknowledged what was happening. "My eyes have just been opened," he confessed. "I believe God wants me to stay in El Paso."

"It's God," I reassured him. "I didn't say anything earlier, Danny, because the decision had to come from you. When hard times come, you'll know in your heart that the calling came from God, not from Freddie, and it will give you strength to hang in there."

We had stopped at a street light. "You see that wino leaning against the wall?" I pointed. "He may very well be your song leader. That drug addict on the corner is perhaps your Sunday-school teacher. You've got your entire congregation right here in the streets of El Paso," I smiled. "Go for it, Danny. Tell them about Jesus, get them saved, and then disciple them for ministry in Jesus' name."

\*　　　　\*　　　　\*

Our congregation was already too large for our storefront church. I had found an old Methodist church on Buena Vista Street for sale, but they were asking the gigantic amount of $100,000 CASH! Common sense told us it couldn't be done, but I knew in my heart this was the church God wanted to give us.

When our people heard, they responded to the challenge. Everyone got involved. The men and teenagers held car washes. The children sold candy and cookies. The women held bake sales, sold *tamales*,[e] and arts

---

[e] *tamales* – seasoned corn dough, filled with spiced, chopped meat, wrapped in softened corn husks and steamed

and crafts. Manuel Zertuche organized the ex-addicts in three shifts, selling *"raspas cristianas"*– "Alleluia snow cones" in the *barrios*.

In the middle of all the activity, our children's church burned down! No one was hurt, but the newspapers picked up the story, and the three major TV stations gave it coverage. The entire city of San Antonio responded. We even received money through the mail from beer joints. Their customers had seen the news on TV, passed the hat around, and sent their donations.

Early in the new year, we were able to purchase our new Victory Temple. God had provided over $77,000 cash, and Christian businessmen signed the promissory note to cover our $23,000 loan. No one but Jesus could have moved some of our city's most prominent business leaders to back up a bunch of ex-drug addicts. "All praise, honor, and glory is Yours, Lord Jesus," I prayed. I was excited!

Our congregation numbered six hundred and was growing. People were coming from all over San Antonio, not just addicts and alcoholics and their families but people of all backgrounds. I took my disciples aside and reminded them, "Jesus told His followers to 'go' and 'make disciples of all the nations.'[10] We are called to disciple men from all walks of life, whether they come to us as drug addicts or 'squares,' whether they live in the streets or a mansion—all men are slaves of sin 'til Jesus sets them free.

"But the larger number of people coming into the church has created a problem," I went on. "Newcomers to our church can easily get lost in the crowd. We

---

[10] Matthew 28:19 (NASB)

want all to feel welcome, so we're gonna start Home Fellowships in the *barrios* all over town. These will be small groups of eight to ten new members and their families. They will get to know each other while studying the Bible together. Then when they come to church, they will at least know someone from their fellowship.

"You set it up," I turned to Luis "Perú." "Give it your best, but break the routine once a month. Plan a special activity: a *barrio* rally, a backyard drama, movie, or picnic."

"Sounds good," Luis was excited. "But where am I gonna get all the teachers?"

"We'll use the guys who are being discipled to become pastors," I explained. "Home Fellowships will be their training ground. Under our supervision, each disciple will, in fact, be 'pastoring' a mini-church. What we do in Victory Temple, he will do in his mini-church. His job will be to meet the spiritual needs of his Home Fellowship members: follow up on them, preach, make altar calls for salvation, pray for the sick, administer the Lord's Supper, and so on.

"All we've taught him through discipling, he will now have the opportunity to put into practice on a small scale. We release him enough to let him test his call to pastor, yet we'll be right at hand to help him if he has a problem he can't handle."

"I'll get on it right away," Luis was all for it.

"Go ahead," I encouraged him. "But I want you to get Mike Hernández involved in there, as a teacher. God's given him a pastor's heart; the problem is, he's afraid of failure.

"Mike told me he wanted to be used of God in any area of the ministry except as a pastor. I didn't argue with him. But listen, Luis, just put him as one of the Home Fellowship teachers. Without Mike realizing what's happening, we'll be discipling him as a pastor. We must never lose the vision of what God called us to do: 'Go' and 'make disciples!'[11]"

---

[11] Matthew 28:19 (NASB)

## Chapter 12

# The Cry of Battle

Then the Lord said to Moses,
"Why are you crying out to me?
Tell the sons of Israel to go forward."

Exodus 14:15 (NASB)

"Hello?" I picked up the phone.

"Freddie?" the familiar voice sounded far off. "This is Marcos."

"Marcos!" I was pleased. "How's the work in Austin? You doing all right?"

Marcos cleared his throat. "That's what I'm calling you about, Freddie...I've blown it. I mean, I can't handle it no more. The temptations, the pressure of the ministry, plus my own family problems—It's too much, Freddie. I'm walking away from it all. I just called to let you know."

"*Cálmala*,[a] wait Marcos!" I tried to encourage him, "Don't walk away from Jesus. I know it gets hard, but let me send someone to pastor the church in Austin so you can come to Victory Temple for a while and restore your strength in the Lord.

"When the 'storm' is over and you're okay, you can pick up where you left off. Hang in there, Marcos, I'll back you up; just get a hold of Jesus."

"It's too late, Freddie," his voice sounded discouraged. "I've made up my mind."

"Come home, Marcos," I insisted. "I know what I'm

---

[a] *Cálmala* – Calm down.

telling you."

"Maybe later, Freddie, but not now," he was regretful. "I don't wanna leave the Lord's work unattended, so you better send someone to replace me right away."

That same evening, during our church service, I motioned David Pérez to follow me outside. I knew he was making good money as an aircraft mechanic; now was the test of his calling into full-time ministry.

"How would you like to pastor in Austin, Texas?" I asked, giving him a quick run-down of the situation. "I can't promise you a big salary, just headaches and heartaches. But you'll have the thrill of seeing the power of Jesus Christ heal broken lives, and that's worth it all."

Without blinking an eye, David smiled, "*Yo le pongo*—I'll do it, Freddie. I'll give two weeks' notice at work first thing in the morning, and meanwhile, I'll start packing." He shook my hand and embraced me. "Don't worry, Freddie, in Jesus' name, Austin will continue to have a Victory church and a Victory Home."

I marvelled at God's power—David Pérez, one day head usher of Victory Temple, next day a pastor in Austin, Texas!

"Marcos' defeat is ours," I shared with Ninfa. "We're gonna have to do something. Our guys are out there in different cities, going through their trials and struggles. We have to let them know they're not alone."

"I remember when we first started here in San Antonio," Ninfa sighed. "There were times that doubt and discouragement almost beat us. Now they're going through the same thing. Is there anything we can do?"

"They're our spiritual children, and it's our responsibility to help them," I nodded. "We need to bring them in to San Antonio at least once a month, or else we'll have more casualties like Marcos. I'm gonna call Juan Rivera and tell him to get on it right away."

That Saturday our six pastors came, eager to fellowship with each other. I greeted them. "Marcos' recent walking away from the Lord hurt us all; that's why I've asked you to come. I believe we've all experienced times of discouragement, times when we've doubted our calling, just like Marcos. That's why I feel so strongly that we need to start coming together for a monthly pastors' meeting. It will be a time to share not only our victories but also our burdens and failures, a time to encourage each other, be ministered to, and be strengthened in the Lord."

Juan Garza spoke up, "What you're saying, Freddie, is in line with the Scripture. The Apostle Paul says, 'Let us not give up meeting together...but let us encourage one another....'[1] Fellowship brings God's family closer together, and we are a family. The blood of Jesus Christ shed on Calvary makes us brothers."

Juan turned and faced the guys, "Here on earth, God has given us a spiritual father in Freddie. He has nurtured us in the ways of the Lord. We were all raised in the same 'cradle' at Victory Home. We grew up as brothers—the more reason to come together and help each other."

"Lack of fellowship creates a breakdown in God's family," I agreed. "In the very beginning of this ministry, I made the mistake of allowing Ramón to start a work in El Paso. He was too new in the Lord and so far away that we didn't maintain the fellowship. We lost contact, eventually lost him, and the ministry he

---

[1] Hebrews 10:25 (NIV)

had begun failed.

"You may think you can make it as a 'Lone Ranger,'" I warned them, "but don't be deceived. We'll always need each other's fellowship 'til Jesus comes."

"Thank You, Jesus!" David Pérez hollered, "Alleluia!"

They began to praise God, and I lifted my hands and joined them, "Alleluia! Praise Jesus; yes, amen–praise Him." Our voices blended as we prayed and sang in tongues. The sweet presence of the Holy Spirit filled the room, and the love of Jesus Christ saturated our hearts, uniting us with Him and with one another.

I reminded them, "This is what Jesus meant when He prayed for His disciples '...that they will be of one heart and mind, just as You and I are, Father–that just as You are in Me and I am in You, so they will be in us....'[2]"

Our first pastors' meeting was a blessing to all. We knew in our hearts this was what the Lord wanted us to do–to live God's Word through our fellowship, love, and concern, one for the other. From then on, we started to meet the first Saturday of every month.

\*          \*          \*

It was soon apparent that the monthly pastors' meetings were an essential part of the continuing discipling process of our pastors. They came ready to share their problems, confess their struggles and doubts, and find encouragement in sharing with each other. There was strength just in knowing they were

---

[2] John 17:21 (TLB)

not alone in the struggles; all were experiencing similar problems. When one of our pastors found a solution through prayer and God's Word, what had worked in his city could be implemented in another.

Each month I had ready a new supply of books and tapes. I was using them with my disciples in San Antonio, and I shared them with the pastors who came to the monthly pastors' meeting. Each pastor left with a grocery bag full of new material—eager to study, make book reports, and share with his own disciples.

The monthly meeting was the "family reunion" we needed to strengthen the ties of love and brotherhood. It kept our pastors in the other cities in touch with what was happening in our growing "family" in San Antonio. The "younger" disciples who were ready to launch out, felt more secure; they knew they could draw from the experiences of their "older" brothers who were already out there.

As a fellowship, we were now more confident in reaching out to new cities. All our people were in prayer for the cities of Texas. We would sense a burden for a particular city. Perhaps it would be triggered by a story in the news about a drug bust in that city or by one of the addicts in Victory Home telling of his burden for his hometown.

During the monthly pastors' meeting, we would again pray for that particular city before sending out an advance team to scout out the land. With at least 50,000 pamphlets in hand, their orders were not to come back 'til all the literature had been distributed in beer joints and among the junkies. That was our usual "first assault" on a city in the name of Jesus.

Sometimes junkies reacted immediately; they accepted Christ and returned to San Antonio with our team. Others called later or just showed up at our doorstep. When the response from a city was strong, we knew it was time to establish a work there. Once a city had been "targeted," we launched out a pastor; his wife already had been discipled in different areas of ministry.

Ninfa had first begun discipling the women; most were mothers of small children. They were trained first to care for, cook, and clean, not only for their husbands and families, but for the guys coming in from the streets. A pastor's wife was also discipled in office work, children's ministry, teaching Bible to other women, and puppet ministry for the elementary schools.

Yolanda Muñoz, a member of our church, had volunteered to work full-time in the office. So Ninfa discipled her. Yolanda became the bookkeeper for Victory Outreach of Texas and began discipling the wives of pastors in keeping books.

\*         \*         \*

Gradually our monthly pastors' meeting had grown, as more men were launched out to new cities. We now had eight churches in addition to Victory Temple in San Antonio, and our eight pastors were beginning to bring their own disciples along to the meetings. I was beginning to think we needed to hold conferences in San Antonio for all the Victory family at least twice a year. I mentioned it to the guys and all agreed.

When I told Ninfa, she listened with interest, then

suddenly burst into laughter. It was a while before she could speak. "I'm sorry, Freddie," she struggled to catch her breath. "It's just that I got to thinking back to when the Lord first touched our lives; all we wanted was to get free from drugs. No one told us anything about being a pastor or a pastor's wife. Now look what we're into! Conferences?"

"I don't know much about conferences," I chuckled. "But I know God is dealing with me about holding them just as He dealt with me about pastoring, so I'm gonna do it."

The following day Juan Rivera returned from El Paso. I'd given him the task of going out periodically to the cities where we had planted churches. He would preach and teach, check on the ministry's needs, and let me know how we could help.

"God is moving up there, Freddie," he reported. "The name of Jesus is being uplifted. Danny and I discussed what you said about holding conferences. He's really for it, and so are all our pastors out in the field."

"Thank You, Jesus," I was excited. "This will give the people in all our churches—men, women, teens, and kids—a chance to see for themselves the fruits of discipling and to catch the greater vision of going out to make disciples.

"The conferences need to be set up to *give practical teaching* from the Bible," I told Juan. "They must *encourage* and *build us up* in the faith, *strengthen* the unity of our family in Christ, and *give direction* so we won't sidetrack from what the Lord called us to do."

Juan Rivera smiled broadly, "Our pastors are ready, Freddie. They figure they're out in the battle-field all year, and they need to come and sit at the

Lord's table and feast on His Word."

"Then let's go for it, Juan," I determined. "This first conference will be in English; six months later, we'll have one in Spanish. I'll talk to Pastor Sonny and Ruben Reyna, Wayman Mitchell and Jack Harris—men that are planting churches and have experience in holding conferences. We'll invite them to be our speakers. We'll kick back and learn from them. Then, when we set up our Spanish conference, we'll know what to do." Without further delay we set out to make the arrangements. Our target date was three months ahead.

\*         \*         \*

Ramiro Torres, one of the older residents of Victory Home, stopped by to see me. He was Manuel Zertuche's disciple and one of his staff counsellors. "Freddie, for over twenty-six years of my life I was a junkie," he reminded me. "I can't keep quiet about the miracle Jesus did in my life. I've got to tell it."

Ramiro's face was kind, but a long scar on his cheek told of his violent life in the drug world. His hair and mustache were turning gray, but his eyes were alight with enthusiasm. "Could I get a couple of months off and take some pamphlets to go testify in Lubbock? There's a lot of junkies hurting in that city...I'll be back in time for the conference."

I knew he was ready. "Go and testify, check the city out, and pray about opening a Victory church and a Victory Home there. Pray about it, Ramiro. If the Lord gives you the green light, we'll launch you out."

"Amen!" Ramiro shook my hand. "Amen!"

\*         \*         \*

Conference time finally arrived. From all over Texas, pastors, their wives and children, their disciples, and members of their congregation joined Victory Temple of San Antonio for a full week. The "Banquet Table" of the Lord was set: Prayer, praise, worship, testimonies, and instructive sermons filled our morning and evening sessions.

During one of our coffee breaks between sessions, José Luis Flores stopped me. I asked him, "How are you and Juan Garza doing in Laredo?"

"God is in it," José Luis was enthusiastic. "He's opened doors to the jail and schools, and the church is growing. God is really blessing, Freddie."

"When are you going out on your own?" I challenged him.

"That's why I stopped you," he grinned. "This conference is just the encouragement I needed. I'm ready to go!"

"Have you prayed about any city in particular?" I asked. "Maybe Corpus Christi?"

He was startled by my question. "Corpus Christi's been in my heart. How did you know?"

"'Cause I know there's a great need and God wants to move there," I replied. "Wanna take it?"

"*¡Seguro!*–Sure!" He shook my hand. "Amen."

"Good. We'll launch you out and support you financially for a year while you concentrate on telling people about Jesus."

After Thursday's morning session, Ramiro Torres approached me, "The Lord's really been dealing with me about opening up in Lubbock, Freddie."

"Are you ready to go and pastor?"

"I'm ready," he smiled. "I'm gonna open up a Victory church and a Home in Lubbock. But here's my problem. The people in La Mesa, just a few miles away, want me to start a work there too; my heart goes out to both cities."

"Go to Lubbock," I advised him. "Get the ministry established. When you're ready to move to La Mesa, leave one of your disciples pastoring in Lubbock. We'll back you up financially for a year; by then you should be self-supporting. I'll help you with books, tapes, and pamphlets for as long as you need it. Tomorrow is the last day of the conference," I added; "we're going to anoint, lay hands on, and pray for you and the other pastors that are being launched out."

After the Friday night service, Ninfa and I were exhausted but happy.

"I cried when the new pastors came up on the stage to be prayed for," Ninfa admitted. "I thought of when José Luis Flores and Ramiro Torres first came to Victory Home, their minds and bodies wasted by drugs. They had failed in everything they tried to do, but look at them now. José Luis launched out to pastor in Corpus Christi and Ramiro in Lubbock."

I smiled at her. "I thank God for all our pastors and for their wives who are willing to go with them wherever God calls."

\*　　　　　\*　　　　　\*

We had already begun to plan the Spanish-speaking conference. "Our theme will be 'Laying the Foundation,'" I told Juan Rivera, "and you and I will be speaking. The other speakers will be those of our pastors who are producing disciples; they are the ones who have something to share."

\*　　　　　\*　　　　　\*

"Hello, Dad," Ricky walked into the house early one morning.

"Hello, son," I was both glad and surprised to see him. "Care to have a cup of coffee with me?"

"Sure do," he made himself at home.

"How's your sister Sandra doing?" I inquired. "Haven't seen her for some time."

"She's doing fine, Dad. She's working 'cause she wants to get herself a car."

"And how about you?" I asked. "What's new?"

"I really came by to let you know that I've enlisted in the Army," he smiled proudly. "I'll be leaving this coming week for Fort Leonard Wood, Missouri."

"The Army? Why not the Marines like your brother Frankie?" I teased.

He grinned, "No, Dad. Frankie don't know, but the Army's where it's at!"

We both laughed and I told him, "Listen, Ricky, when your brother Frankie joined the Marines, he came by before leaving for California. I asked him to go see Papa, to let him know he had enlisted. It made Papa's day; he talked about it for weeks. He was so proud that his grandson was in the military service. Now I'm gonna ask you to do the same, Ricky. Papa has always been patriotic, and he was an Army man himself. Go see him before you leave."

Ricky smiled and nodded, "Sure will, Dad."

When he got ready to leave, I encouraged him to seek the Lord. I told him, "Let me pray for you, Ricky, like I did for Frankie, that God will keep His hand over you and that one day you'll give your life to Jesus."

\*　　　　\*　　　　\*

"Mom! Dad!" Josie and Paul crashed into our bedroom. "Our brother Jesse came to the teenagers' worship service! He accepted Jesus as his Savior!" Josie gasped for breath, "And he said he was going to start coming to the church services."

"Did you get to talk with him? What did he say?" Ninfa asked anxiously. "Did he like the church?"

"He didn't say much," Josie replied. "He was very shy around us."

"He was just a baby when we left him," Ninfa explained. "Even though he's our son and your brother, we've been strangers to each other for nearly eighteen years. Let's continue to pray that Jesus will bring us together as a family. He is the only One who can do it."

One evening, a few months later, our phone rang about 10:00 p.m. Ninfa answered. A few minutes later, she walked back into the room: "Freddie, it's Jesse...he wants to come home!"

*       *       *

The Spanish-speaking conference was as successful as our English-speaking conference had been. These biannual "family reunions" became the high points of our year. From conference to conference the attendance multiplied. We could no longer have our services at Victory Temple but had to rent a school auditorium to hold the crowd. The highlight of our conferences was always the launching out of new pastors and the response of others feeling the call to be discipled for ministry to a new city.

During one of our Spanish conferences, Luis Salazar pulled me aside, "I've discipled George Fernández.

He's ready to take over the children's church. It's time for me to return to my country," he grinned broadly. "Lima, Perú, needs a Victory Temple and a Home. God had already started to deal with me about it," he explained, "but this conference confirmed it; my people need to hear about Jesus."

Ninfa and I were assuring Luis of our financial support for at least a year, when Mike Hernández joined our conversation. "I want you guys to train me," he blurted out. "God is calling me to pastor."

"You've already been prepared!" I chuckled. "All the time you've been teaching in the Home Fellowships, you were being discipled to pastor."

"You mean, I'm ready...?" he gasped. "Now?"

"Houston, Texas, has an urgent need," I suggested. "Interested?"

"If you think I'm ready," he smiled, "I'm interested!"

Danny Ibarra from El Paso was right behind Mike. He had fifteen disciples with him. "This is Freddie García," he introduced me. "He's your spiritual grandfather." He then pointed to the fifteen, "Freddie, out of this group, six have a pastor's heart, and I'm discipling them already. They have expressed a desire to pastor a *Templo Victoria*–Victory Temple and a Home in Juárez, Mexico!" Danny was elated, "They'll be ready to be launched out during our next conference."

"Thank You, Jesus," David Pérez broke in. "I'm discipling two guys. One will start a new church right in the city of Austin; the other is still praying about what city to go for."

"I've got three disciples too, Freddie," Juan Garza grinned. "When they're ready, God willing, I'll send them to pastor south of the border."

José Luis Flores raised his hand to catch my attention and shouted, "I'm discipling too, Freddie. I have faith I'll be launching out four pastors!"

One by one they told of what God was doing in their cities; about the changes Jesus was making in their own lives; about how their disciples were growing—in knowledge and in number—and starting to disciple others. I listened in silence as they talked, gratitude swelling within me. I had not shared with anyone my inner fear that my disciples would not reproduce and launch out disciples of their own. If they had not reproduced—I would have failed. The vision would have stopped with me. But they had caught it! This was the vision coming true, the evidence that Jesus was in charge.

"Praise Jesus!" I lifted up my hands, "Let's praise His wonderful name!" Immediately the room was filled with sounds of worship as they all joined me in prayer, the beautiful blending of different languages, uplifting and glorifying the name of Jesus.

After prayer the guys continued sharing with each other, talking about their plans for the following months. "Hey, Ramiro!" Danny called him aside. "I'm having a men's breakfast meeting in six weeks; I'd like you to be the speaker."

"Sure!" Ramiro smiled, "I'll be glad to. I'd like you to come and speak at my church also. When can you make it?"

The rest of the guys were all exchanging speaking engagements. I smiled and stepped over to Ninfa who had been watching and listening. Together we walked out the door. I knew they wouldn't miss us for a while. "It's time we let them go," I told her. "They are ready to incorporate on their own."

Ninfa smiled, "Oh boy, wait 'til they hear that. I hope they'll understand it's for their own good."

She had done the paperwork when we first formed a nonprofit corporation, and I added, "I want you to be present at the next pastors' meeting so you can explain what they need to do."

I called the pastors and told them to come without their disciples this time. The meeting was held at our home. There were twenty of them, and we all sat around the sixteen-foot-long, dining-room table. I started by talking about the "proprietorship mentality."

"That's when you think something belongs to you—when in reality it belongs to God," I told them. "We need to be careful. Don't make the mistake of thinking that our disciples belong to us; they belong to Jesus. Sometimes we have trouble in releasing them. We figure we've worked for years with this guy, and just when he's ready to be of help to our ministry, he wants to go. We're left alone—back in square one without anyone to help us—so we begin to hold them back. That's the proprietorship mentality, and it's wrong! If that was the way to do it, I'd have the biggest, best-organized church in town 'cause I'd still have you guys with me."

I could tell they were wondering what I was aiming at. "That is not what God called us to do," I continued. "God told me a long time ago: 'Work with them, disciple them, and when they can stand on their own feet, release them. Release them and you'll keep them. Try to keep them and you'll lose them.'

"I didn't understand what Jesus meant at first, but I obeyed and let you go," I smiled, "and I haven't lost you. You may be in other cities, but the bond of love between us keeps us together. You don't have to come to these pastors' meetings; no one is forcing you. You come because it is in your heart to do so. Why do you continue to show up for the conferences year after year? 'Cause you want to. But if I had not released you at the beginning, you might have walked away angry, upset that I did not help you come to your 'fullest potential' in Christ Jesus. That's what Jesus meant when He impressed in my heart, 'Release them and you'll keep them; keep them and you'll lose them.'"

All around the table they were smiling and nodding. I caught Ninfa's eye and cleared my throat before going on: "Do you guys understand where I'm coming from?"

"Amen!" they all voiced approval. "Amen!"

"Good!" I smiled. "'Cause now I've got to talk about letting you incorporate on your own."

There was a hush in the room and they listened, motionless. "When you were new in Christ, the responsibility of caring for you was mine. I taught you from the Word of God; I saw to it that you were fed, clothed, and housed. You were my spiritual sons. Now you are men of God with responsibilities of your own. You are spiritual fathers.

"Even when you were first launched out, doing a work for God in your own cities, I still carried the responsibility of financing you 'til you could stand on your own. And those of you who are now financially independent are still under the Victory Outreach of Texas umbrella. However, the time has come to release those of you who are standing firm and to let you incorporate on your own. This way, I can have more time to work with your younger brothers who are just starting out."

None of them spoke. They looked at one another, then at me, in disbelief. Ninfa broke the silence, "They don't understand, Freddie. They think you're trying to get rid of them." She turned to face them, "That's not it at all."

"No!" I stood up from my chair, "on the contrary. I'm not cutting you loose; we're still family. This isn't gonna divide us; it's gonna keep us together. Everything will be the same. We'll still have pastors' meetings and conferences. I'm still gonna financially support for a year each pastor that I launch out. And when your disciples are launched out, you will help them stand on their own feet and then release them also. We're family; we'll always be family. But you need to incorporate on your own. It's for your own benefit."

"But, Freddie," David Pérez stood up, "I don't want to be independent; I want to be under your leadership."

"You will, David. I'm still your spiritual father. I'll always be. Nothing has changed. I'll still keep giving you guys books and tapes to help in your ministry. If any of you get in a hole financially, we'll bail you out. But listen, David, this is not gonna be a denomination. It's a fellowship, a family. The thing that binds us together is our love for each other in Christ. You'll still be in the Victory Fellowship family, but you're gonna be here because you wanna be.

"Jesus said: 'By this all men will know that you are My disciples, if you have love for one another.'[3] The thing that binds us together is not legality—it's love." The guys were quiet, looking at each other, smiling, nodding. You could almost reach out and touch the

---

[3] John 13:35 (NASB)

love of God right there in the room.

"I'm with you, Freddie," David Pérez grinned. "Thank You, Jesus! *¡A Dios sea la gloria!*[b]"

One of the newer guys began to clap his hands. Another, then another joined in. As if on signal, we all stood up; we knew we were in the presence of the King of Kings. The applause grew louder and louder 'til it thundered in reverent praise.

Slowly, the applause diminished as the gentle sound of prayer in tongues rose and got louder. Our hearts were overflowing with gratitude. We knew that "He who began a good work in [us] will perfect it ['til] the day of Christ Jesus."[4] We uplifted His name and gave all praise, all honor, and all glory to Jesus Christ, our Lord—the source of our living and our reason for going on!

---

[b] *¡A Dios sea la gloria!* – To God be the glory!
[4] Philippians 1:6 (NASB)

# Chapter 13

# The Night Cometh

I must work the works of Him that sent Me,
while it is day:
the night cometh, when no man can work.

John 9:4 (KJV)

Every time the double door leading to the Intensive Care Unit swung open, my heart skipped a beat. Close to midnight all my family members had gone home, exhausted after a day of anxious waiting. Only Ninfa and I remained. Prepared for an all-night vigil, we had brought along a big thermos full of hot coffee. Ninfa carefully laid out our brand-new sleeping bag on the floor, behind the now-empty Information Counter. "Lie down a while, Freddie," she coaxed me. "You've got to take care of yourself; remember your recent heart attack."

At exactly 3:00 a.m. the nurse came out. "You better call all the family," she advised. "She's taken a turn for the worse." Immediately Ninfa went to the pay phone and called my sister Santos. She in turn would call the rest of the family including my two sisters Estella and María who had flown in from California as soon as they heard that Mama had been hospitalized.

It all happened so suddenly. Monday afternoon Mama had complained of a mild chest pain on her left side. After doctors diagnosed it as a heart attack, she was taken immediately to the Intensive Care Unit.

Wednesday she suffered a second heart attack.

Friday, at exactly 4:00 a.m., the doctor came out to the waiting room and told the assembled family that Josefa Lucio García had suffered her third and final heart attack. My kind and loving mama was dead.

Many of the relatives broke down and started sobbing, but I was stunned by the pain of losing Mama. Quietly, I walked across the hall to the windows and looked out into the darkness, praying in the Spirit.[1]

*Mama's gone*–the thought kept reeling through my mind. *She's really gone!* But just as I thought I'd break down, a calmness enfolded me. Ninfa had followed and stood beside me. Gently she slipped her hand into mine. "It's almost 5:00 a.m.," she whispered. "Let's go home."

"She's right," Santos joined us. "Go home, Alfredo. Don't worry about the funeral arrangements; we'll take care of it and let you know. You've got to get some sleep, or you'll get sick. Don't forget your heart condition."

Still holding hands, Ninfa and I took the elevator down to the first floor. We walked in silence through the long, empty hospital corridor to our car. We slumped on the front seat. I could feel the pounding of my heart.

Ninfa broke the silence. "You told me years ago that when the time came for Mama to die, you wanted to rent a room somewhere by yourself, away from everyone...Remember?" When I didn't answer, she continued, "...I guess what I'm trying to say is that if you feel like doing it, Freddie, go ahead. Don't worry about what people will say, or about explaining anything to anyone. You just do what you feel you must do."

---

[1] 1 Corinthians 14:15 (NASB)

"No, Ninfa...," I replied. "I'm all right. Years back when I mentioned that to you, I didn't think I would be able to handle my grief any other way than to be alone.

"But do you know what I'm experiencing right now, Ninfa, even though Mama's gone? An overwhelming peace. I can't explain it, but I feel the Holy Spirit so close to me. In the middle of my hurt and sorrow, God is comforting me. I've known Jesus as my Savior, my Healer, and my Lord, Ninfa, but never have I experienced the reality of the Holy Comforter[2] in such a powerful way–I feel His peace within me."

*"Gracias a Dios,*[a]" Ninfa was relieved. "I've truly been worried about you."

"Don't worry," I assured her, "I'll be all right. How about you? You okay?"

"I'm okay," she sighed.

"Then let's go home."

As soon as we got to the house, I walked straight to the bedroom and lay down. The morning sun was struggling to break through gray clouds. I felt a great heaviness and closed my eyes.

*       *       *

Ninfa's hand stroking my hair woke me up.

"How you feeling?" she handed me a cup of coffee.

"Have I slept long?"

"Twenty-four hours," she smiled. "It's Saturday morning. You needed it, after all those sleepless nights at the hospital."

Her words brought me back to reality. It hadn't

---

[2] John 14:16 (KJV)

[a] *Gracias a Dios.* – Thanks be to God.

been a bad dream—Mama was really gone.

"Santos called to say that Mama's body will be ready at Max Martínez Funeral Home today at 1:00 p.m. She's to be buried Tuesday at Fort Sam Houston Cemetery."

"What about Papa, Ninfa? Does he know?"

She shook her head, "He forgets what we tell him right away, so the family has agreed not to say anything."

"That's good," I nodded. "He's lost sense of time and reality anyway."

"Besides," Ninfa sighed, "he's bedridden and there's no possible way he could be moved to attend the funeral. Sick as he is, it would kill him to find out Mama's gone. Before I forget," she added, "Juan Rivera and Manuel Zertuche came by. They said to count on them for anything you need done."

"Phone them," I told her. "Tell them we're gonna hold church services at the funeral home for the next three nights. I want them to go right now and get everything ready for tonight; set up microphones, speakers, musical instruments, the works. Tell Paul to take the electric piano, and ask Josie to sing. Mama loved to hear them both. I want Paul, Josie, you, and the Victory Temple Band to sing praises to our Lord every single service. The name of Jesus is gonna be glorified.

"I'll preach tonight. Tell Manuel he's to preach Sunday night. Juan Rivera can take over Monday night. Tuesday morning when Mama's body is taken to Victory Temple, I'll preach at the worship service there and then at the cemetery. We prayed for Jesus to heal Mama, Ninfa, and He's answered our prayers. Mama's not dead—she's completely healed and alive in Christ

Jesus for all eternity."

"Thank You, Jesus," Ninfa's eyes were moist.

All day Saturday, friends and relatives came in and out of our home. They brought everything from flowers to homemade breads, from cookies to full-course meals; all were expressing their love and concern.

"You know how Mama always set the example of attending all funeral services of friends and acquaintances," Ninfa reminded me.

The thought of it made me smile, "I even used to tease her about it."

"Well, now I understand why she did it," Ninfa confessed. "Each person who has come by has helped us get through the day with less pain just by their fellowship."

That evening, when we drove up to the funeral home, our Victory Temple ushers were supervising the parking lot area. Dressed in their red berets, red shirts, and black pants, they were ushering the people into the chapel.

As I walked in, my heart was lifted. There stood Juan Garza from Laredo, José Luis Flores from Corpus Christi, Danny Ibarra from El Paso, David Pérez from Austin, and all the rest of the pastors with their wives and disciples. They didn't have to say a word; I knew we'd learned to be a real family, one big family united through the bond of God's love.

The funeral home had given us their largest chapel, and people were standing along the walls and overflowing into the halls. The ushers counted four hundred present, and the abundance of flowers surrounding Mama's coffin told of what a friend she had been to many. I preached about Jesus that night, and I felt as if Mama, from her heavenly place, was rooting for me, "Tell them, son...tell them about Jesus."

At each of the church services we held at the funeral home, people came forward and accepted Jesus as their Savior. On the last night, one of the mortuary employees came forward and surrendered his life to Christ. I rejoiced in my heart, *"O death, where is thy sting? O grave, where is thy victory?"*[3]

Tuesday morning, as Mama's body was slowly lowered into the ground, I reflected on her life: She was born and raised on her father's farm in San Marcos, Texas. It was there she met Papa. He had been hired as a field worker to help harvest the crop. They fell in love, and he asked for her hand in marriage. Their wedding was in 1923, and that same year they moved to San Antonio.

"As far back as I can remember, Mama," I whispered, "you fought to keep your family from losing their heritage by simply living our culture, making your *tortillas,*[b] *caldo,*[c] and *tamales,*[d] constantly reminding us to use our Spanish language.

"When you met Jesus as your Savior, Mama, you came to believe that the healing of our people would come through Him. You were right. Black is beautiful...Brown is beautiful...White is beautiful...if you've got Jesus in your heart. You taught us by example, Mama; now it's our responsibility to carry on."

\*                    \*                    \*

---

[3] 1 Corinthians 15:55 (KJV)

[b] *tortilla* – a thin, unleavened pancake characteristic of Mexican cookery

[c] *caldo* – soup

[d] *tamales* – seasoned corn dough, filled with spiced, chopped meat, wrapped in softened corn husks and steamed

Late that night, when the relatives were gone and our kids were finally asleep, I had a chance to talk with Ninfa. "You know my family was always very close," I began. "I can remember when some of our relatives had financial trouble, Papa opened our home to that entire family–I mean children, pets, and all–'til they could get on their feet again.

"But Papa and Mama's kindness didn't stop with the family. When someone in the *barrio*[e] was sick, Mama was always there to help, and she took my sisters along to babysit, cook, wash, or do whatever was needed. Mama believed in unity within the *barrio*, in loving her neighbors.

"When all my sisters and brothers were married, Mama managed to keep the family close. Every Sunday she cooked a big pot of *caldo de res*[f] for the entire family; at Christmas her traditional *tamales*; each New Year, the crispy *buñuelos*.[g] These were the magnets she used to draw her children together. I've applied that same idea in our Victory Fellowship; our pastors' meetings, banquets, and conferences are the 'spiritual *caldo*' that draws our Christian family closer."

Ninfa had been listening and nodding in agreement, and I went on. "Now that Mama is gone, Ninfa, let's make *caldo de res* at least once a month at our home for all the Garcías. For Thanksgiving, each family can bring their own speciality, and we'll provide our traditional American turkey. Let's encourage all the cousins, nephews, nieces, and grandchildren

---

[e] *barrio* – neighborhood

[f] *caldo de res* – beef soup

[g] *buñuelos* – Mexican pastry

to come."

"And at Christmas," Ninfa was excited, "all the García women can come and fellowship during the *tamalada*![h] We'll keep our cultural traditions alive and combine them with our Christian family worship."

"Thank You, Jesus!" I sighed deeply. "Mama would have loved to see it. And one more thing—like Mama—let's never stop encouraging our children to use their Spanish language."

Without delay, the next morning we talked to Jesse, Josie, Paul, and Jubal. "We're aware that you know Spanish. But you're not practicing it," I told them. "You may practice speaking English at school and at church with all your Anglo and Black friends, but here at home when you speak to your mama and me, speak Spanish. That way you will learn to master both languages. From now on, if you slip up and talk to us in English, you will wash the dishes after supper."

They understood and didn't argue; *"Sí,*[i]" they replied. Mama had discipled them well.

Ninfa waited 'til they left the room before speaking. "I believe that what you're doing with our children is right—and very important. It's your family that will give our children the sense of belonging and cultural identity. I can't trace my roots; my real mother died three days after I was born, and my birth certificate reads: 'Father—Unknown.' I have no legacy to leave my children."

"Yes you do!" I quickly reminded her, "God is your Heavenly Father and your family is made up of all the Christian brethren through the blood of Jesus Christ—

---

[h] *tamalda* – tamale making
[i] *Sí* – yes

THE GREATEST LEGACY, THE GREATEST HER-
ITAGE WE WILL BOTH LEAVE OUR CHILDREN
IS THE EXAMPLE OF OUR CHRISTIAN LIFE."

\*       \*       \*

"Ninfa! Have breakfast for me when I return!" I
yelled as I walked out of the house. "I'm going over to
see if Santos needs anything for Papa. I'll be right
back." It was Friday morning; Mama had been gone
exactly one week.

Santos greeted me at the door when I arrived,
"What are you up to?"

"Just came over to see how Papa and you are
doing," I walked in.

"We're okay," she smiled. "I just left his room to give
him a little privacy. He's on the bedpan. Let's go to the
kitchen and have a cup of coffee with Estella while we
wait."

"She still in town?" I was surprised. "I thought she
was already back in California."

"I was worried about Papa," Estella had heard me,
"so I decided to stay a few more days."

Just then, my niece Linda came out of her room and
walked to the kitchen sink to get a glass of water. "It's
for Papa," she explained. "It's time for his medication."

"Let me help you," Santos got up and followed Linda to Papa's room. Within seconds I heard a commo-
tion and turned just as they re-appeared in the kitch-
en doorway. Santos' face was ashen. "Papa's not
moving," her voice faltered. We all rushed to the
room. Santos called out, "Papa! Wake up, Papa.
Answer me."

Papa's eyes were open, but I knew the breath of life

had left him. "Leave him be, Santos," I tried to make her understand.

"No, Alfredo," she argued, "Papa sometimes doesn't answer 'cause he can't hear very well...Papa," she shook him, "Papa!"

Gently I took her arm and pulled her away from the bed, "He's gone, Santos. Papa's gone."

I called Ninfa and within minutes she arrived. Without speaking she came and stood by me. She had already called the funeral home, and an hour later, two attendants carried Papa's body out on a stretcher, covered by a white sheet.

"*Ay,*[j] Alfredo," Santos sobbed. "We lost Mama only a week ago, and now we've got to go through it again with Papa."

"The comfort we have," I consoled her, "is that he accepted Jesus as his personal Savior. Both Papa and Mama are in heaven."

She wept softly, "I've got to let the family know, then go make the funeral arrangements."

"I'll go with you," I volunteered. "Papa was a true patriot; he loved and believed in America. I want him to have all the honors of a soldier who loved and fought for his country: the twenty-one gun salute, the bugle call, the works. I'll pick up the bill if necessary."

"There's no charge, sir," the gentleman behind the desk smiled. "We just need to know who'll be receiving the flag at the cemetery the day of the funeral. It belongs to any one of his children still living with Mr. García at the time of his death."

My brothers and sisters were all present, but when no one said anything, I spoke up. "That would be you,

---

[j] *Ay* – oh

Santos, but if it's all right with you, and if the rest of the family doesn't mind, I'd like to keep it...May I?"

"I'm for giving it to Alfredo," Estella answered first.

*"Seguro,*[k]*"* Santos agreed. "You can have it, Alfredo."

One by one my brothers and sisters consented.

*     *     *

...holding the American flag tightly, I watched Papa's coffin as it was lowered into his beloved American soil. I could almost hear him whisper in my ear, "Son, this is the legacy I leave to you—my American flag. I believed in it, loved it, fought for it, and would gladly have died for it."

"America, with all its faults, is still the best country in the world, Papa," I whispered. "Here I have the freedom to preach the gospel of Jesus Christ and to serve and worship the Living God."

"Freddie," Ninfa touched my arm, "let's go home and pack. We've got *The Junkie* presentation in Houston tonight, remember?"

"Let's go," I agreed. "We have buried Mama and Papa, but we must go on. '...The Lord gave and the Lord has taken away. Blessed be the name of the Lord.'[4]"

*     *     *

The Houston Music Hall seats more than 3,000 people, and to our surprise, it was full.

"How you feeling?" Ninfa asked me backstage.

---

[k] *Seguro* – sure

[4] Job 1:21 (NASB)

"Can you go on with the performance?"

"Papa and Mama have gone to be with the Lord," I answered. "I'm gonna miss them...but I have the assurance we'll be together in heaven."

"Amen," she smiled. "Thank You, Jesus."

"Then let's get to it," I grabbed her hand. "Let's tell those people out there about Jesus."

Juan Rivera was Master of Ceremony. He opened the meeting with prayer and then introduced me.

"We buried my beloved mama a week ago," I told the audience. "This morning at ten o'clock we buried my dear papa. But we're here tonight because Jesus lives in our hearts. We came to tell you that He's real, and He loves you." The applause was thunderous.

"And now, please welcome my wife and family." Ninfa and Josie stood with me on stage; Paul was at the piano with the Victory Temple Band. In the side wings, the actors were waiting. Along the walls and aisles of the Music Hall, I saw the familiar red dresses of our usherettes, the red shirts and red berets of our ushers.

Ninfa sang first, then Josie; their faces shone with an inward light; their eyes glistened with tears. They sang of God's mercy and His power to change lives, and it seemed as if the Lord Himself carried the message to the hearts of their listeners. Never had I sensed so strongly the presence of God with us—strengthening—comforting—filling and surrounding us—flowing out to the people in the packed auditorium.

When the curtain rose on *The Junkie*, the audience was captivated from the first to the last of the six scenes. In the cast were Ninfa, Paul, and I, along with Manuel Zertuche, Juan Rivera, and two other former addicts. The extras were guys from Victory Home. I played the pusher and, in the last scene, the preacher. The story was simple; we acted out the life of a junkie.

At the end of the drama, I turned to the people and introduced the cast: "Each one of these men you see before you are not actors; for forty-five minutes they have merely re-enacted their lives for you. They were once stoned-out, hard-core drug addicts. What you see tonight are living miracles, living trophies, telling of God's power to change lives.

"Listen to me, folks, the miracle that took place in our lives didn't happen when we called upon the name of Socrates, Charles Darwin, Karl Marx, or Sigmund Freud. This transformation took place in our lives when we called upon the name of our Lord and Savior Jesus Christ. It was He who broke the shackles of sin and drug addiction and set us free. We have no alternative but to give all the praise, all the honor, and all the glory to Jesus Christ, the Son of the Living God!

"This same Jesus is here tonight, and the miracle that happened to us can happen to you. All you have to do is come forward and ask Jesus Christ to forgive you for all of your sins."

The presence of the Holy Spirit filled the vast room and people got up from their seats and started coming. A sense of awe filled me as I watched them; many were weeping, hands uplifted. They came right up onto the stage and fell to their knees, calling on the name of Jesus. Others crowded in the side wings, down in front, and in the aisles. All were calling on Jesus Christ to forgive them for their sins. From the very back of the auditorium, a Black woman cried

out: "I see angels! The whole stage is full of them!"
She ran down the aisle—"I see angels! There's angels
up there!"

Late that night we finished loading our small station wagon with the few props we used in the drama.
I hugged Ninfa, "Come on, let's go home."

The night was calm and clear, and bright with
stars. The road stretched before us, and I could relax
at last. "We have a lot to be thankful to Jesus about,"
I reached over and touched Ninfa's hand. "He's been
so good to us."

"Really good," she sighed deeply. "He's brought us a
long way from when we bummed around on Guadalupe Street."

Silence engulfed our thoughts momentarily, and
then I could no longer hold back what was in my heart:
"This morning, Ninfa, when Papa's body was laid to
rest, I became more aware than ever of the responsibility I've been given—Mama gave me a love for my
heritage; Papa gave me a love for America, and God
has given me a love for Him.

"Jesus set me free not only from enslavement of
drugs and racism, but from self-hate. I'm free to love
my Mexican heritage without being disloyal to America; I'm free to love America, without rejecting my
Mexican heritage. Free to accept my very own special
identity: Mexican-American.

"As a Mexican-American, I hurt when I see our
people living a life of bondage and self-hate. My heart
aches when I see them putting themselves and others
down.

"As a Christian, I must tell them that what causes
division, strife, and misery among men is not race,
culture, language, or class, but sin and rebellion.

That God's love, through Jesus Christ alone, embraces every race, nationality, culture, and language, for we are all created in His image. Jesus Christ does not remove ethnic and cultural differences. He reconciles them!

"That's why I'm compelled to preach the gospel of Jesus Christ, and make disciples for Him 'til the day I die, for '...the night cometh, when no man can work.'[5]"

---

[5] John 9:4 (KJV)

# Epilogue

Our Victory Fellowship now numbers forty churches: thirty in Texas, nine in Mexico, and one in Perú. Most of them already have Victory Homes of their own. Several disciples are in training to be launched out, some as far as Puerto Rico, Venezuela, and Spain. Most of our forty churches are incorporated; others soon will be. The churches are planted in the barrios in the poorest sections of town and still operate on a shoestring budget, most often in storefront buildings. We help them as much as we are able; the Victory family still pulls together, and anyone in need can count on being helped.

Our conferences regularly draw over a thousand in attendance, twice annually. Our Spanish-speaking conference is held in January, our English-speaking conference, in July. In addition, José Luis Flores in Corpus Christi, Danny Ibarra in El Paso, and Ramiro Torres, now in La Mesa, are holding conferences in their own cities for those in their churches who are not able to travel to San Antonio.

Our youth caught the enthusiasm of the conferences and asked to have their own. At our monthly pastors' meeting, I told the guys: "Many of us focus on the drug addict and the alcoholic—and we must never lose that vision—but there is a whole generation of young people who need to be reached before they become casualties of addiction. Prevention is better than rehabilitation. Our youth are the future leaders of our fellowship."

We decided to hold an annual, three-day youth conference during the summer, just before the beginning of school, and a one-day rally during Christmas vacation. The aim is to strengthen our young Christians, prepare them to face the peer pressure on the campus and in the classroom.

Our first youth conference drew four hundred young people. Juan Rivera and Johnny Zamarripa, our Youth Director, led the sessions, and our teens in discipleship training were speakers. They challenged our young people to take the gospel of Christ to their unbelieving schoolmates.

Our first women's conference was held in English with three hundred women in attendance for three days of meetings. Our second conference, in Spanish, drew five hundred. Our women's conferences are now held in April and in October.

Drama is an essential part of all our conferences and of our ministry. It is an effective teaching and evangelistic tool. *El Bule–The Bully*, a drama on peer pressure and drug abuse, was written by Johnny Zamarripa. It is performed in schools and jails, at civic clubs, on front lawns, in parks, and on the streets. It has even been presented in the chambers of the San Antonio City Council and on the courthouse steps. A video-taped presentation of *El Bule* is also used by our teams who teach drug prevention in various schools and prisons. More than a dozen plays have been added to our list, many of them written by the young performers themselves. Another effective tool is the short comedy skits performed by our "clown ministry." All of our dramas tell the message of salvation.

Elementary schools asked me to develop a program on drug prevention for the children who are too young to benefit from lectures. It was then that the idea of a puppet theater came to life. The story of "Little Mary Jane who introduces Freddie to her family of harder drugs" has been shown in most of San Antonio's elementary schools with good response. Our puppets are popular in churches and neighborhoods as well. New material has been added, and during the summertime, our nine- through twelve-year-old kids are the eager puppeteers.

The music ministry is growing also. In addition to the album made by our ex-addict choir, "The Ballad of San Antonio," telling the story of our work in the city, has been recorded in Spanish and placed in juke boxes throughout Texas. The Spanish version of "The Ballad of Freddie García," will be placed in beer joints, and the English version will soon be released. Ninfa's album, taped "live" at Victory Temple, is in Spanish. Josie recorded her album in English, and Paul is releasing one of his own in English this year.

In June 1984, they called us from Mayor Henry Cisneros' office. I was asked to appear at a meeting of the City Council. I was there with my family, the girls from the office, my disciples, Nando Flores, and all the guys from the Victory Home. I watched the men file in, clean shaven and neatly dressed. At one time or another all had been "guests" in city jail or the state penitentiary. They had added to the problem of drugs and violence for the city and the state. Now they came to witness to the solution.

Mayor Cisneros called me to come forward. He then read a proclamation, recognizing me as *"Benefactor de la Comunidad"*–Benefactor of the Community:

"This extraordinary City earned its position among America's unique cities because of the many contributions made in the past by special people like you. Our present City is nothing more and nothing less than the sum of all these efforts.

The Mayor and members of the City Council commend you for the many years of service to the community. Your example of determination and hard work to free first yourself, then others, from enslavement to drug addiction has set the best example possible that a love of God and a firm belief in one's own self-worth can work wonders in today's society. Your dedication and Christian Outreach to others is truly a firm sign of victory over adversity. At this time, the Mayor and City Council call to the attention of all the citizens of San Antonio your very important contributions and hereby proclaim you as

### 'BENEFACTOR DE LA COMUNIDAD'

The community owes you a great debt of gratitude. You should always take great pride in knowing that you have joined the ranks of all eminent San Antonians who have made this City such an exceptional place with such a bright future. In witness whereof, I have hereunto set my hand and caused the seal of the City of San Antonio to be Affixed this 14th Day of June, 1984.

Henry Cisneros, Mayor."

The ceremony was carried live on television, and I had the opportunity to tell who the *real benefactor* is, the One who changed my life and the lives of the men who were with me—*JESUS CHRIST*—the only lasting solution to the problems of human pain and suffering, in the city streets, at home, or at City Hall.

Our story continues. Daily, Pablo "Risas" Torres and Ramón "Lembo" Ibarra take their teams to the streets, the beer joints, the jails, and the hospitals; Johnny Zamarripa takes his teams to the schools. Daily, men, women, and young people show up on the doorsteps of Victory Home, where Nando Flores is Home director. They will never be turned away—even if all we can offer is a bowl of beans and a mattress on the floor. The riches they find in Christ Jesus, however, cannot compare to any treasures on earth.

San Antonio, Texas, October 1987
Freddie García

If you would like to know more about Freddie García's work or would like to be part of his ministry, write to him at:

> Freddie García
> P.O. Box 37387
> San Antonio, Texas 78237